Homecamp

*Stories and Inspiration for
the Modern Adventurer*

Doron & Stephanie Francis

Homecamp

*Stories and Inspiration for
the Modern Adventurer*

Contents

Why we go

....

You may have felt it before. A surge of joy, a feeling of wholeness, a spontaneous connection to something greater than yourself. Those moments when the sun sets or rises, sitting quietly by a mountain or the sea. There might be a shiver down your spine, an emotional shift – a kind of release. It's perfectly normal, this feeling. It's called experiencing nature. That connection is a sense of belonging in the natural world.

For many, that feeling seems like it's slipping ever further out of our grasp. For the first time in history, more people live in urban areas than not. As our opportunities to experience nature grow narrower, it seems no coincidence that stress, obesity, anxiety, attention disorders and depression are on the rise. There is even a name for it: Nature Deficit Disorder, summed up by the range of behavioural issues that arise when human beings, especially children, don't spend enough of their time outside.

Technology isn't helping matters. It has become embedded in our lives, and with it the so-called 'attention economy' works hard to vie for our time and attention. Some studies suggest that, on average, we check our devices a mind-boggling 85 times a day. Paradoxically, the connectivity our phones and computers seem to promise us has left us feeling less plugged in to each other.

That said there has been a broad shift in attitude, particularly amongst the young who see digital detoxing as a natural and necessary reaction to our over-mediated, over-curated lives.

Science is catching up to what we intuitively know: that time spent in nature – the more, the better – has a positive effect on our wellbeing. It decreases stress, lowers heart rate and blood pressure, increases creativity and promotes clearer thought. Enter the modern phenomena of therapeutic camping programs; forest kinder for kids; tech-free retreats; city planners putting 'green' space at the heart of their designs and doctors prescribing their patients a walk in the park.

The journey that led us to Homecamp – our blog, store and, now, this book – came from our own experiences retreating from our plugged-in lives and rediscovering the simple joys of being outdoors.

Over the years, we have been lucky enough to go on some epic adventures. We hiked in South-East Asia and the Andes;

explored the depths of the Amazonian jungle; watched bears in one of Russia's most remote corners; and travelled around our native Australia and New Zealand. But it was a camping road trip to California's High Sierra and coastal Big Sur that inspired us to create Homecamp. Somewhere in the grand meadows, amongst the giant sequoia trees, we fell in love with the idea of starting a brand centred around the idea of inspiring people to get outside, exploring our world's many beautiful places without leaving a negative imprint behind. We were frustrated with the modern concept of buying products that would break within a couple of uses only to be replaced without question, creating endless waste for landfill. When we camped, we wanted useful, well-designed products that would last us a lifetime.

Homecamp is not about aspiring to travel to far-flung places, becoming an elite outdoorsperson or conquering the wild. It's about celebrating a simple truth: you don't need to be *doing* anything to connect with nature. It's about how just *being* in nature is enough.

This book is about adventurous everyday people – photographers, architects, chefs, writers, builders, seekers, thinkers, risk-takers – who are reuniting with nature in diverse ways, and with transformative results. Their stories all start with a desire to connect with the world around them, to step out of the daily grind and find a different, wilder, less trodden path. Their stories prove that getting back to nature isn't as hard as you might think.

From alternative ways of living – in a van, or a shipping container, or a house made of hemp – to being alone in the woods, biking across continents, gazing at stars and surfing through frigid waves, these stories are all about inspiring you to spend more time outdoors. Maybe you've been meaning to take that camping trip with friends, or maybe you've been dreaming of a life on the road.

Perhaps you are looking for inspiration on how to start your own outdoor movement. In these pages, we think you'll find the push you need.

For us, camping is a fun and easy gateway to nature. Almost anyone can camp. It's inexpensive, and a realm in which learning a few simple skills opens up a broad range of adventures. Finding and chopping wood, making a fire and cooking a meal on its hot coals are activities almost as ancient as humanity itself, and hugely satisfying. Our how-to guide will get you started on developing these simple skills and planning your own adventures, whether they be in your backyard or off in the bush.

Homecamp is all about finding new ways to switch off, create meaningful experiences and a heightened connection to the Earth. As contributor Alastair Humphreys says, 'Adventure is an attitude' – one we humbly hope to inspire.
..........x

Doron & Stephanie, founders of Homecamp

Homecamp is an outdoor lifestyle brand that aims to inspire people to get outside and experience nature as much as possible. Launched in 2014, Homecamp has built up a loyal legion of followers and customers who want to enjoy the outdoors equipped with products and skills that will last a lifetime.

“
Homecamp is all about finding new ways to switch off; to create meaningful experiences and a heightened connection to the earth.

The rewards of awareness

When renowned photographer Christopher Phillips caught a bacterial infection called meningococcal during a trip to Bolivia, it changed his life. Struggling with treatment and recovery back home in Australia, Christopher started to practise meditation. It transformed not just his healing process, but his life and work. He found that his meditative practice made him a better photographer: his attention was heightened, his senses sharper, his patience wider. He now leads workshops on meditative photography in natural spaces.

The idea of combining meditation with nature and photography came to me after I contracted meningococcal. I had volunteered to work at an animal refuge in the Amazon basin, and I picked up the bacteria through the water supply.

Upon returning to Australia, I spent two years being treated by Western medicine with little results. So I started on an alternative therapy journey, which introduced me to Ayurveda medical practices and meditation.

My first week of meditating created both a mental and a physical shift. My body felt like it was cooling down after a lifetime of being agitated and out of alignment. My mind felt like it was quietly opening and relaxing, allowing me to see aspects of my life that had been hidden, into parts of myself I hadn't been able to see before.

This experience had profound implications for both my photography and my daily life. Whenever I meditated before the beginning of a shoot, I noticed myself becoming aware of far more than I had previously. I had a feeling that I was becoming part of each moment in a direct and connected way. My patience was extended, my vision heightened and my connection with the subject intensified.

I continued experimenting with this mix of meditation and photography and found that being in nature amplified my feeling of connection. Nature has fewer distractions and more invitations to be curious and engaged in the moment; the feeling of connecting with nature's patient, nonresistant vibrancy allowed me to tune in. The more I practised, the more this quality became part of my day-to-day.

I started getting up before dawn to drive to a national park, leaving just enough time to meditate in my car before the first rays of the sun appeared. Slowly, I'd begin exploring the new landscape, allowing all the sights, sounds and smells of the forest to lull me out of my mind, immersing me completely in the experience of observation. These sessions of meditative practice in nature left me feeling relaxed, focused and fulfilled.

> **"**
>
> Nature has fewer distractions and more invitations to be curious and engaged in the moment; the feeling of connecting with nature's patient, nonresistant vibrancy allowed me to tune in.

The focused awareness required for photography allowed me to penetrate more deeply. I noticed that it added structure to my practice, further refining my awareness so I could drop even more deeply into the moment. I refined my awareness so that my focus was on the fundamental elements of photography: highlights and shadows, colour, form and texture. To keep myself anchored to the present moment, I would continually bring my awareness back to the sensations of my body, starting with my hands, feet and the places where my clothes touched my body. As I became more focused and sensitive, I refined it to just the sensation of my breath entering and leaving my nostrils.

My feeling of being acutely aware began to strengthen; I could focus on what I was photographing, but I also had another level of consciousness that was observing everything I was doing. This regular practice of taking time to quieten my mind, to remove the judging, analytical side of thought and settle into nature's vibrant frequencies began to create changes. Not only in the quality of my photography, but in the quality and depth of my connection to life.
..........X

"

I'd begin exploring
the new landscape,
allowing all the sights,
sounds and smells of
the forest to lull me out
of my mind, immersing
me completely in
the experience of
observation.

Home is where you park it

Mitch Williams became obsessed with Volkswagen vans after watching classic '70s surfing movies. He always dreamed of the van life, planning how he would make the bed, how he would maximise the storage. He eventually purchased a classic four-speed column-shift manual 1978 Nissan e20 van, and after making it into a functioning tiny home, lived in it with his girlfriend. They winnowed life down to its simplest pleasures and material necessities, woke to the sunrise every morning and balanced time in nature with his day-to-day life as a graphic designer in Melbourne, Australia.

Tell us about your van.

Growing up I was obsessed with Kombi vans. Every Christmas and birthday I was swamped with Kombi-related mugs, cushions, t-shirts, key rings – even a Volkswagen hub cap. I was looking seriously at getting a van for about a year before I bought the 1978 Nissan e20, doing research and talking to mates with vans. The only thing I knew was that I wanted it to be retro (preferably '70s), just like the ones in the old surf movies I love, like *Morning of the Earth* and *The Endless Summer*. Those guys were living the dream.

The van runs really well for its age, even though it sometimes struggles getting up hills and going into reverse (the gears are pretty sticky). It's one of those motors that you drive by how it sounds and feels. If it's revving heaps, you back it off a bit and let it coast; if your seat starts heating up, it means the motor's getting hot – talk about '70s heated seats! It's frustrating at times, but that's the beauty of these old things. Treat them right and there's no reason for them to stop running.

What inspired you to get a van?

Well, the old surf films. And I really loved the idea of pulling up along the coast and waking up to check the surf every morning without getting out of bed. It's like having a beachfront house at all of my favourite surf spots. A room with a view – who wouldn't want that?

Have you spent any time living in the van, and how did it change the way you live?

Right after I bought the van, my girlfriend and I lived in it for two months on a farm in the Yarra Valley in Victoria, Australia. We loved waking up to the sunrise, no alarms; the sun would shine right through our window and we'd just wake up! Moving into the van meant we had to ditch almost everything we had down to strictly what we'd need on a day-to-day basis: some clothes, a couple of pairs of shoes, speakers, skateboards, surfboards, wetsuits, a guitar, a coffee grinder and a French press. Not to mention the little things to make it as homey as possible: plants, incense, books, pictures and *don't forget the mosquito spray!* Becoming a full-time van lifer and living the simple life is quite liberating; it's super humbling being surrounded by everything I need to be happy.

What's the best moment you've had in the van?

We've had so many awesome moments in the van. I'll always remember the first trip we took, down the Great Ocean Road. It had been my dream to drive it in my own van and it was surreal to actually be doing it: stopping and surfing when we found a wave and setting up camp with the views we'd only ever enjoyed in passing. It was a killer start to having the van.

What does van life mean to you?

Van life is all about not being tied down to one place. It's constantly being on an adventure and enjoying the things you really love. Van life is the ultimate freedom. For me, it became about letting go of my long-term plans and taking a step back to see my future from a different perspective. It's stressful at times, but allowing life to happen and being able to roll along with it (literally) is so much more exciting.

Being able to go with the flow opens up so many opportunities. I'm picking up new hobbies on the road: cooking, hiking, biking, exploring, popping into vintage stores and op-shops to find unique things for the van, photography, film, reading and road trip singalongs. Van life has made me appreciate those little awesome moments in life that you take for granted or that are easy to forget about: cooking outdoors, seeing sunrises and sunsets, rolling out of bed and instantly being outside (which really wakes you up), using candles for light and not just for smell, and falling asleep gazing up at the stars.

..........x

"

Van life is all about not being tied down to one place. It's constantly being on an adventure and enjoying the things you really love. Van life is the ultimate freedom.

> "
> It's like having a beachfront house at all of my favourite surf spots. A room with a view – who wouldn't want that?

For van lifer Mitch Williams, living out of a van means he gets to wake up, roll out of bed and find himself at some of his favourite beaches, including ones along the Great Ocean Road outside his hometown of Melbourne, Australia.

Cleaning up the coast

Natalie Woods had probably cleared hundreds of pieces of rubbish from beaches before. But the first piece of rubbish she remembers hauling off the sand was an old bread tray, washed up on a beach far from any bakery. She was searching for meaning at the time, looking for new ways of living outside of her 9-to-5 job. After picking up this one piece of plastic, Natalie started seeking out beaches strewn with rubbish – the sort avoided by regular beachgoers. She cleared one beach, then another and another, the stream of rubbish seemingly endless. Inspired, she co-founded the Clean Coast Collective – an organisation committed to cleaning up Australia's coastline – with her partner, Daniel Smith.

We never set out to start a beach cleanup organisation, or to clean beaches at all.

I'm not even sure why we picked up that first piece of rubbish – it can't have been the first we'd picked up on a beach, but it was the first that stuck in our minds. It was a brown plastic bread crate – the type you would see at your school canteen, piled high with fresh bread rolls. But this one was covered in barnacles and was on a beach. It had obviously been at sea for a while and, without thinking, we just picked it up and started dragging it back with us.

We were at a point in our lives where we were seeking something more fulfilling than our 9-to-5 lives. We were stuck in the daily grind, working Monday through to Friday, then escaping to the beach on the weekend. The same thing, week after week, until we found that one piece of rubbish.

From that point on we became strange people, driven to find dirty beaches and clean them up. It was like a treasure hunt: looking at maps of the coastline to see which beaches might be the most affected, observing the swell updates not for surf, but for the next southerly, which would bring more plastic ashore. Speaking to locals along the coast, who recalled tales of beaches covered in plastic. 'Oh yes,' they would say, 'some friends hiked there and they said it was covered in fishing buoys! It was around that headland, but I'm not sure exactly where …'

To those around us at the time, I'm sure it seemed like we'd lost our minds. Perhaps it even seemed like a noble pursuit, to be devoting so much time to the land and sea. But we got just as much out of it as the environment did. We had an excuse to explore further than we had before, seeking out new beaches and new stretches of coastline. In the beginning it took us to new beaches in our local area. Eventually it took us around Australia's entire coastline.

During our beach cleanups, wandering the sand for hours on end, we found ourselves drifting into almost meditative states. Sometimes we would wander together, chatting about this or that, but for the most part we would head off in different directions, letting the ebb and flow of the rubbish take us away on our own adventures. Our minds would drift from our daily checklists and soon be drawn into our present surroundings … 'doesn't the air smell salty today?', or 'how crunchy the sand feels beneath my toes', or 'I've never seen a sea urchin that colour before'.

> **"**
> The task of searching for rubbish pulled our minds into the present, distracting us from the 'real world', just for those few hours.

There was no reason to stress or angst over an email that had to be sent or a task that needed to be done. We were too far from our computers for that to matter. The task of searching for rubbish pulled our minds into the present, distracting us from the 'real world', just for those few hours.

At times we would cross paths with old salty seadogs: men who had lived and breathed that coastline for almost a century, who would gruffly mumble, 'You're wasting your time. You won't be able to clean up this mess'. We would just smile and continue on our way. Perhaps they had a point – perhaps the problem was too big for us to fix.

But … surely there's no harm in trying?
..........x

"

Sometimes we would wander together, chatting about this or that, but for the most part we would head off in different directions, letting the ebb and flow of the rubbish take us away on our own adventures.

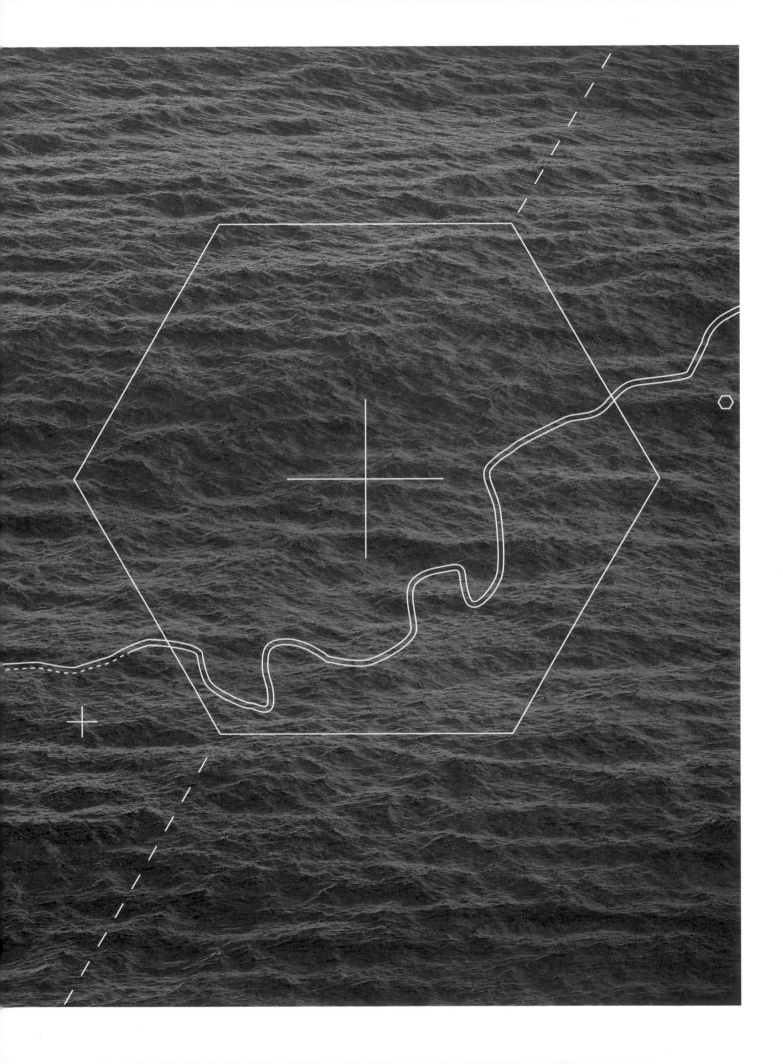

Finding the path

Ashley Hill had no hiking experience when she decided to walk the Pacific Crest Trail in North America. Her mum had recently died of cancer at the age of fifty-five, and Ashley needed space to grieve and room to grow. She knew she had to follow her dreams and live her life to the full, no matter how crazy it seemed. So she set off southbound, walking from Canada to Mexico on a solo trip that was meant to take six months. Three years later, Ashley is still hiking, still adventuring and still discovering herself along the way.

What is the Pacific Crest Trail (PCT) and what made you decide to walk it solo as your first adventure?

The PCT is a slice of perfection. It is roughly a 4265-kilometre (2560-mile) trail from Canada to Mexico that passes through Washington State, Oregon and California. The route traverses twenty-five national forests and seven national parks, from scorching deserts to snow-capped 4000-metre (13,123-foot) mountains. I hiked solo to help me process my mother's passing. I was looking for solitude and struggle, to grieve and grow. The idea of being alone in the wilderness just seemed so therapeutic.

How did you find the experience as a solo hiker?

It was everything I was looking for and so much more. It became my zen. I never feel alone when I'm out there; it connects me so much more to the world, nature, community. Ego dissolves and I feel like I become part of something. I rarely get scared, either. This surprised me, coming from the city and being such a social human in my old life. Sure, there are times when I wish that I could share the sunset or a spectacular view with a loved one, but I have my camera and have made friends with my shadow, so there you go.

You go by the name Bloody Mary on the trail. How did you come by it?

It's a tradition on American thru-hikes to be given a trail name for something silly you've done. Hikers often take the name up as a kind of new identity, forgoing their birth name entirely.

I used to suffer from a condition I like to call 'drunk feet', where I would fall on average three times a day. I was just so distracted by all the mountain beauty! So my legs were a bloody mess in the beginning. I was coming into my second resupply town to load up on food, covered with duct tape bandages and dried blood stains of pride. I asked the staff at the diner if I could get a bloody mary, and they renamed me on the spot!

What made you decide to keep adventuring after coming off the PCT?

Thru-hiking changed my life. I discovered so much about myself, while realising how little I knew about the world around me. When I finished the PCT, I was in a perfect position to continue on; I had quit my job, moved out of my apartment, detached from all bills and most material possessions. I had discovered something that brought me immense peace and joy. I learnt that I was an incredibly capable being and had a new belief that I could do things I never considered possible before.

After tackling the PCT and the Pacific Northwest Trail, you made your way to New Zealand to walk the Te Araroa (TA). Can you describe that hike?

The TA is a 3000-kilometre (1864-mile) route that spans the length of the country's two main islands, from Cape Reinga in the north to Bluff in the south. It starts on the seemingly endless 90 Mile Beach, followed by a mountainous mud pit of extreme fun! You'll find yourself wading through rivers for days on end, then frolicking across hilly farmland with the sheep. There is an eight-day paddle down the Whanganui River and risky mountain passes that will have you wondering if you'll make it out alive. Then there's the fact that about thirty per cent of the route is on paved road, literally bisecting major cities and residential areas. I see the Te Araroa more as a journey across a country than a trail ... a journey with unique challenges at every corner.

When Ashley Hill started going on thru-hikes, she discovered a pastime that made her feel strong, grounded, challenged and at peace. Though she expected to feel lonely out on her own, she found that being alone made her more open to the joys of the trails she walked like the Te Araroa in New Zealand.

How did you find walking in the landscapes of New Zealand as opposed to North America?

Challenging! I love a challenge, so it was a wonderful experience, but trails in New Zealand are definitely more extreme than the more established routes in the United States. Switchbacks, where a trail zigzags back and forth up a mountain to make it easier to climb, don't seem to exist in New Zealand. You simply go straight up and over, giving us hikers some rock-hard, superhuman calves! And why worry about building a trail beside a river when you can just walk through it for hours on end? I will never forget the mud … mud up to my thighs at times.

But then, the TA is extremely well-marked, making navigation much easier than on other routes I've hiked. Plus, the route has a spectacular hut system that provides welcome refuge from the weather. You can experience four seasons in one day on the hike. Hypothermia and drowning are big killers in the back country, so these huts are a wonderful thing to have. I struggled with all the road walking, but, all in all, the Te Araroa was an amazing experience and I wouldn't change a thing.

You've talked about your love of cowboy camping. What is that?

Cowboy camping is my favourite discovery in the outdoor world. It's simply sleeping under the stars without a shelter overhead. It took me nearly a month to build up the courage to finally try it, but since that day, I only pitch a shelter under threat of rain or snow. I am in love with stargazing and have a bucket-list goal to spot a UFO. I'm also quite lazy, and this method reduces my setup and cleanup time to nearly nothing.

What are the most satisfying moments of a hike?

When you realise you've been smiling from ear to ear for ninety straight days. When you start to use the moon's cycle as a calendar. When you forget what you look like because it has been so long since you've encountered a mirror. When you can identify the flavour of water; I never knew that fresh spring water bursting out of a mountain has the best taste on Earth. When you start your day at three in the morning, headlamp lighting your way, just so you can walk into a sunrise. Oh, just about everything on a hike is satisfying!

How do you manage to keep your pack lightweight on thru-hikes?

Redefining necessity is the first step to going lightweight. When I pack for a trip, I start with what is essential to survive: shelter, sleeping system, water purification system, navigation system, clothing, first aid kit and a pack to carry it all in. Then I try to lighten each of these things. For example, I cut my toothbrush in half and cut off all tags, zipper handles and pockets from my clothes. I trim unnecessary straps from my pack and cut the borders off my maps to save weight. Then I try to get multiple uses out of my gear: dental floss and a needle double as a sewing repair kit; my tarp is also used as a rain poncho so I don't have to carry an extra jacket. For everything else, I ask myself if it is worth its weight. A stove is a luxury item. I can survive on cold food, but that won't be very enjoyable, so I carry one with pleasure. Soap and deodorant – nope, I'll take a shower when I get to town!
..........X

> **"**
>
> I discovered so much about myself, while realising how little I knew about the world around me.

"

I was looking
for solitude and
struggle, to grieve
and grow. The idea
of being alone in
the wilderness
just seemed so
therapeutic.

The conviviality of a bonfire

Karri Hedge could mark the passing of time with her yearly bonfire. It always happened just as the season was tipping over into winter, before the bone-stripping chill descended. The invites were sent to family and friends, calling them out to the Australian country, where Karri and her family would have spent weeks forming a giant structure made of branches.

All sorts of friends gathered: those who were comfortable in the country and those who rarely left the city; groups and couples and families. Once the bonfire was lit, all barriers and pretensions fell away. New friends scrambled about, lobbing more kindling onto the fire, and old friends chatted and burned mementos, drunk on wine and the entrancing power of the flames.

The invitation always said they should wear their warmest clothes. But every year, I worried that someone wouldn't understand just how cold it gets out here. So we gathered old coats and hats and scarves into a pile, just in case.

The week before the bonfire, I'd become an obsessive weather-checker. Seven days out, the rain would be predicted to be torrential, the winds gale-force, and I would despair. Six days out, the storm would have moved forward a day and we were going to be okay! Five days out, the gloom would descend again. Three days out, you could generally rely on the forecast, but it didn't stop me praying for a late game-changing miracle.

I don't know why I worried about the weather, year on year. The party happened regardless. Sometimes we huddled inside around the stove, hiding from the rain, and sometimes we sat outside, marvelling at the crystal-clear sky sprayed with stars.

There is something intimate and exhilarating about a fire in the darkness.

When the time came, rain or not, we always made our way along a lantern-lit path to the towering pile of branches at the back of the property.

My dad would call the local fire brigade the afternoon before to notify them about the fire – the responsible thing to do. 'That's right, two cubic metres', he'd say, with a wink to me. It was more like twenty.

Friends who were there for the first time would make their way with old timers through the unknown darkness until they were told to stop. They had no concept, yet, of how high the stacked branches towered above them – where the pile began or ended.

The newspaper and firelighters, tucked into nooks and crannies by the light of a phone, would be lit. They flared promisingly, and we whooped and cheered. Yet these fires always burnt themselves out, leaving nothing but a few twigs glowing in the darkness.

Dad would go and get the kerosene. It never worked, but he always went to get it anyway and sprayed it liberally, splashing it over gumboots and into mugs of wine. It made a satisfying *WHUMPH* when it was lit, and then, predictably, it fizzled out. Every time.

Tactics were discussed. A better, drier spot found amidst the pile and the lighting process repeated: newspaper, firelighters, matches. On the other side of the pile, a rival team's fledgling fire would crackle into view, spurring us on. We tended our new fire, feeding it lovingly with dry twigs and leaves.

Some people were content to watch. Some were directors, arguing about the dampness of the wood or the direction of the wind. Then there were the doers. They brought headlamps so they could find the driest kindling at the bottom of the bonfire, and climbed right into the pile to reach it. They worked tirelessly, feeding ever-greedier flames until they became self-sustaining.

The flames would take hold, climbing quickly, lighting up the surrounding faces with an orange glow. The ring of watchers retreated gradually, all turning like lambs on a spit, as they warmed themselves in the fierce heat.

There is something intimate and exhilarating about a fire in the darkness. Couples huddle together, watching the flames – eyes shining, arms intertwined. Children dart in and out of the surrounding trees, revelling in the intermittent freedom from adult eyes. The more daring ones poke at the flames with long sticks, giggling at the shower of sparks they send flying into the air. A roar of solidarity might ring out as someone throws a symbol of a troubled past into the fire: a ritual sacrifice for a new beginning.

As the fire dwindled, people would dribble back towards the house to refill drinks or put the kids to bed. Eventually everyone followed, drunk on fire and wine. There were games and songs into the early hours.

In the morning, we'd walk back to the bonfire site. 'The walk seemed so much longer in the dark!' someone would say. We would round the corner to see a circle of ash, still smoking gently.

As people left, they might pass my dad in the driveway with the chainsaw out. He'd wave them off and return to his sawing. Already working on next year's bonfire.

..........X

> "
> A roar of solidarity might ring out as someone throws a symbol of a troubled past into the fire: a ritual sacrifice for a new beginning.

Every year, Karri Hedge and her family would invite their friends to gather around a bonfire on their property. Sometimes they would throw old mementos into the flames – symbols of a troubled past, burned with hope for a new beginning.

Riding through hardship and on to joy

When Dan Marsh started dreaming of going on a solo bike journey, he initially planned to ride from Melbourne, Victoria to Lake Eyre, South Australia – a journey of more than 1000 kilometres (620 miles) into Australia's harsh desert centre – to photograph the sun-cracked salt plains of the usually dry lake. But after months of dreaming and planning, he thought to himself: why stop at Lake Eyre?

Dan left Melbourne with everything he'd need strapped to the back of his bike. He headed south along the surfers' coastal route towards Adelaide, then left the beach behind to ride up through the centre of Australia and, eventually, across to Queensland's tropical north. It was six months of adventure, a solo ride characterised by the generosity of the people he met along the way and the grandeur of the landscapes he passed through.

I daydreamed for three years about riding my bike alone through Australia, along the coast and up through the Red Centre. I wanted to travel without time constraints, just camping, surfing, connecting with people, shooting photos and living a footloose existence.

Whenever I told anyone my plans, they'd give me a weird look or say that it didn't really sound like much of a holiday. But I loved camping and riding, and I was obsessed with the idea of this adventure.

It wasn't until a few weeks before I left that I actually started to have fears; before that, I'd romanticised about the adventure rather than actually thinking about what I was getting myself into.

> ❝
> # I realised I was holding on to the struggles – and I just had to let everything go.

The day I rode out of Melbourne, it hit me like a tonne of bricks: everything I'd dreamed about for so long was happening, and it scared the shit out of me. It was overwhelming and surreal riding off with no real thought of when I'd be back, leaving behind a lover and everything else to chase some kind of fantasy, loaded up on a bike so heavy that I could hardly ride it down the street let alone halfway around Australia. What was I thinking?

I definitely wasn't fit or prepared for the experience, but I don't think that I could ever have really prepared my body or mind for what I was about to put it through. I really struggled in the first couple of weeks; my body hurt, the riding was tough, and sleeping on the hard ground in my freezing tent took its toll on me.

But then something kind of clicked. I realised I was holding on to the struggles – and I just had to let everything go. After that pivotal moment, everything became easier. My mind relaxed and all the relentless chatter about how hard everything was seemed to fall away. I became more present with every kilometre, and each day was a joy.

It was funny – once I'd gotten into the rhythm of my new life, it became my everyday reality. From the outside it seemed crazy and wild, but to me it was just … my life. I was entrenched in it, loving every single day. I felt a beautiful sense of freedom that I'd never really experienced before. I was often alone in isolated places, but I never felt lonely; just to sit by myself out in the wild was a special experience.

And I met so many people on the road who helped me out in some way, with beds, meals, showers and rides. Their outright generosity was so heartwarming.

As much as riding thousands of kilometres was about riding a bike and pushing my physical limits, it was also about so much more than that. The road taught me so much about myself, and life in general. I was content living in the dirt, smelly and filthy a lot of the time, but not really caring. Being limited to only what I could carry, I discovered that I loved the simplicity of having very little. Fears come and go, but they're only fears; they're not facts. I learnt that once I pushed past them, anything was possible.

I'm stoked with what I was able to achieve, particularly with the support of my partner, who understood my dreams and desires. When I finally made it to Far North Queensland, she took up the challenge and joined me on the road. We rode down the east coast together, planning to end up in Melbourne … but we made it as far as Byron Bay, New South Wales, and haven't quite left. One day we'll finish the journey. But life's pretty good where we are right now.

..........x

> **"**
>
> Fears come and go, but they're only fears; they're not facts. I learnt that once I pushed past them, anything was possible.

> "
>
> It was funny – once I'd gotten into the rhythm of my new life, it became my everyday reality. From the outside it seemed crazy and wild, but to me it was just ... my life.

A land of ice and fire

As we approached what looked like a former Soviet-period state collective farm, we saw an old Russian Mi-8 helicopter being fuelled and a couple of men tinkering with its engine. The sight of people fussing with the engine of the helicopter in which we were about to fly didn't exactly soothe our nerves. It looked run down, its back doors held closed with a length of string. A tentative-looking way to get to the heart of a rugged, untamed land.

We'd only recently arrived in Petropavlovsk-Kamchatsky, the capital (and only) city in the Kamchatka region of the Russian Federation. Kamchatka is a large peninsula in far-eastern Russia, on the Pacific Ocean north of Japan. An area of some 270,000 square kilometres (about 100,000 square miles), it is sparsely populated. It holds some 300,000 people, most of whom live in Petropavlovsk-Kamchatsky. Beyond the city is a dramatic land — a living place of geysers, glaciers and wild weather, along with 160 volcanoes, sixteen of which are still active.

"

We felt insignificant in the face of a vast horizon full of mountains and volcanoes; a landscape devoid of human habitation. This, we realised, was how Earth once was.

The helicopter was taking us to Kurilskoye Lake on the southern part of the Kamchatka Peninsula, where wildness and isolation reigned. After swallowing our apprehension, we were ushered on board, our luggage stacked in the middle as we sat around on side seats, military-style.

The helicopter flew low, keeping out of the higher altitude winds and staying close to the tundra. We opened some of the windows and saw a vast green land outstretched below us, intersected by streams and with no signs of human life. The horizon was pierced by multiple cones, their tops in the clouds — volcanoes. It had the air of a lost world.

A bit over an hour later, we were dropped off at Kurilskoye Lake. We settled into a newly built, large cabin surrounded by wire fences to keep the local bear population out. The lake is a nature park reserve, and we were there as the guests of two resident rangers. The rangers would get snowed in during winter, but it was late August — the peak of summer — and the temperatures were humid and mild.

The next day we moved north to the nearest volcano, travelling in a six-wheel-drive converted military truck across riverbeds, climbing as far as the truck could take us. Continuing on foot, we trekked the long approach across rising ground and snowfields. The terrain became steeper closer to the top of the volcano. We encountered vents of steam and sulphur, reminding us that the volcano was only slumbering.

When we finally reached the top, we were surrounded by a landscape of ice and fire — a place where the Earth showed its power to change and control its landscapes. We felt insignificant in the face of a vast horizon full of mountains and volcanoes; a landscape devoid of human habitation. This, we realised, was how Earth once was. We felt fortunate to witness it.
..........X

Words by Stephanie and Doron Francis. Images and captions by Alexander Gerasimov, who loves to explore Russia's wild spaces.

The first time I visited Kamchatka it was winter, when the weather is severe and there are no tourists. Upon arrival, I took my tent and went to the shore of the Pacific Ocean. It was there I first met the winter surfers, who surf even when the water is 2°C (36°F), chasing the beauty of a sea surrounded by snow. I stood on the shore, drawn into the meditation of the surfers, the cold and the landscape.

Kamchatka is very far away from Moscow, where I was raised; thousands of kilometres to the east. I dreamed of this primeval place on the shores of the Pacific Ocean, with its volcanoes, geysers and mountains, almost untouched by man. It's a crazy place. Here you can climb to a volcano's crater and surf in the cold ocean, or see a bear or wolverine in its natural habitat.

The sisterhood of the road

There's something about the freedom of a motorcycle: that feeling you could ride anywhere, go anytime. There are no barriers between you and the outside world – you feel it rushing freely past you. It's that feeling that got Ashmore Ellis and Anya Violet hooked on riding, and it's that love that led them to found Babes Ride Out, a female-only moto-camping event in Joshua Tree, California. It started on a whim, an idea to gather a few friends for a campout in the desert: no pressure, no dramas, just riding. But when fifty women showed up for that initial event, they knew they were on to something.

Ashmore, when did you start riding motorcycles, and what do you love about it?

I started street riding when I moved to California and saw so many people on motorcycles. With the weather being incredible pretty much year-round, I picked up a little Yamaha and took a safety class. I love everything about it. Riding motorcycles forces all of your senses to work together at the same time.

I was riding through the Catskill Mountains in New York State recently, and I could see beautiful green, rolling hills; I could smell the earth, cows and haystacks; I could hear the engine roll; I could taste the rain as it started to pour; and I could feel the power of the bike as I flew down the road. For that brief moment, I was experiencing the world in an incredibly different way – one that was unique to my surroundings and that will never be exactly duplicated.

Before you started Babes Ride Out, did you often go camping with your bikes?

I had been quite a few times prior to Babes Ride Out's existence. I learn something new every time I pack it up and head out. Moto-camping can turn anyone into a minimalist very quickly.

Where is your favourite place to ride?

I love the desert. There is something about endless roads and dry, hot air. We've been riding to Borrego Springs, California for years. It's about an hour-and-a-half away from my home and features some of the best riding roads I've ever been on.

What happens at a Babes Rides Out campout?

We ride motorcycles. This is not an event for those who just want to party all day; the site shuts down and you are expected to get out and ride several routes, which we have curated for all skill levels. At night we have live bands, karaoke and a mechanical bull-riding contest.

"

I was experiencing the world in an incredibly different way – one that was unique to my surroundings and that will never be exactly duplicated.

" I love the desert. There is something about endless roads and dry, hot air.

Babes Ride Out has become more than an event – it's a real community. What's the community like?

Thousands of ladies of all ages on different bikes who love to ride, camp and connect. We originally made it ladies only so we could all hang out with zero distractions and truly connect. Nothing makes us happier than seeing these ladies so excited just to be there.

What would you say to someone who is scared to ride?

If you are truly scared, riding motorcycles may not be for you. Motorcycles are extremely dangerous, and riding is a personal choice you need to make for yourself – not to fit in, stand out, whatever. If you still have the will to hop on two wheels, start on dirt. Eat shit a few times in said dirt, then see how you feel. Still scared? Take a class. Still scared? Hang up the keys and find yourself another hobby.

..........x

A home made by hand

Shane Hurt and Queenie Yehenala trucked a shipping container onto a 20-hectare (50-acre) property near the town of Kinglake in Victoria, Australia, hiding it deep in the woods. The two designers, who met in Shanghai years before, turned this shipping container into a vacation home, built of plywood and paint. It was a chance to use their hands, disconnect from the city and share a connection with family and friends.

You'll need to drive down a bumpy, steep gravel road, and then an even bumpier dirt road, to get to Shane and Queenie's home in the thick forest near Kinglake. There are few remaining tall gum trees here, their trunks black and cracked as a reminder of the fire that tore through this land ten years ago, taking lives, houses and communities. The rest of the trees are striplings, light and skinny, sticking their trunks out with bravado as they reach for the sky.

It was fire that took the original house on the property, a mid-century modern structure with clear views down to the river that is now obscured by upstart gums.

Shane and Queenie's house, placed in a clearing halfway up the hill, is a 6-metre (20-foot) shipping container. They trucked it onto the property as an iron shell, the old company logo still printed on its side.

The container both contrasts and is at home with its surroundings; it's made noticeable by the deck around it and the tools strewn on the ground outside. Over time, Shane and Queenie have turned this shell into a home, complete with kitchen, reading nook, a single bed and a queen bed loft. The interior is simple and striking, befitting its size, with exposed pale wood and black details.

They come here to unplug, to unwind as a family: lighting candles, cooking on a barbecue, washing up in a bucket and slapping away the mosquitoes that slip in through the doors. It's more like camping than a traditional holiday home. The family relax out on the deck, swaying in the hammock, after days spent making a home in the bush.

..........x

"

They come here to unplug, to unwind as a family: lighting candles, cooking on a barbecue, washing up in a bucket and slapping away the mosquitoes that slip in through the doors.

Shane Hurt and Queenie Yehenala wanted a weekend cottage to call their own – something that harmonised with nature rather than something that fought against it. They made it out of a shipping container, creating a peaceful place to unwind.

Night vision

By day, Kate Armstrong's summer camp was a busy, known world. But that world changed overnight, when a group of campers and their counsellors spent the night in the woods after everyone else had gone home. Night transformed their woods from known to unknown, the campers from comfortable to hovering on the edge of fear. But after the campfire was doused and sleeping bags were rolled out, they'd go on a night walk. The rules were simple: no flashlights, no voices. Just sneakers and feet, ears and eyes laid open to the dark.

We would gather along the side of the gymnastics hut. It was just a roof, four pillars and a platform, open on all sides to miles of woods. The campers would inch in close around us counsellors, eyes made huge by the thrill of being the only ones left.

By day, our camp was endlessly loud – filled with the splash and crash of water games and arrows thwacking targets; the rise and fall of singalongs and names being shouted between the trees. These girls were the queens of that daytime kingdom. At twelve, they were the oldest, confident in every step of the path.

"
No one's immune to a fear of the dark. It's built into our bodies, ancient and bone-deep.

But camp was different after the buses left and the sun sank down below the treeline. Night turned our knowable, well-worn woods into something strange and, if we were honest, a little scary. The paths became pale lines swallowed by things we couldn't see.

No one's immune to a fear of the dark. It's built into our bodies, ancient and bone-deep. We fill the darkness with our scariest monsters and every troubling thought we ignore when it's light. That's why our ancestors learnt to light fires and tell stories around them. They wanted to control the darkness – to push it back and out of reach.

The gym had no electric lights – just our flashlights. Without those, the only light came from the moon and, if you squinted, the lichen that glowed around the base of certain tree trunks. These campers were city kids, used to quick and easy ways of dispelling darkness. They had never known a room free of phone glow and street lamp, or the light that creeps in around a slightly cracked door.

Inevitably, one of the campers would ask: *how will we see without flashlights?*

And we would tell them: *you've got to let your eyes adjust.*

Close your eyes, nice and tight. Keep them closed and count to ten. When you open them, don't let them settle on any one thing. Just let them wander and your night vision will come.

When we first opened our eyes, there were just vague shapes and shadows. But then details would start to emerge: the deep grooves carved into the tree trunks; the edges of the pebbles that littered the trail; the bright corners of someone's teeth as they smiled. The stars were brighter, now. Their outlines flickered in our eyes like tiny fires.

We would line up, everyone within an arm's length of each other. One counsellor would walk in front, one in back – the braver job. It was hard to shake that eyes-on-the-back-of-your-neck feeling. Even knowing we weren't in danger, the dark made our senses hard to trust.

No one was allowed to talk, a rule almost as important as the one about flashlights. Light and sound both do the same job: they wrap you up in a self-made universe, blocking out the rest of the world. But we wanted to help our campers strip away that buffer. To show them what happens when you let the darkness in.

In the beginning, the silence was always too much for them. We could feel how badly they wanted to fill it – a familiar laugh or cough to make the darkness feel less like a living thing. But then they would start to hear their footsteps, soft against the dirt of the path. Their heads would tilt towards leaves as they shivered, and towards squirrels overturning the underbrush. The woods would come alive around them, but it didn't feel threatening. It felt more like a secret being shared.

After a while we no longer had to *shhhhh* them. They were too awed by the silence to want to break it apart.

We wound downhill through oaks and poplars. Eventually, we would get down to the lake. The campers would sit along the wooden bridge that led to the kayak shed, looking out over the water and the trees beyond. The longer we sat, the more we noticed: the reflections of the stars on the water and the skating insects that broke them. The chorus of bullfrogs, so haunting and deep. Our breaths blended in, becoming a part of the forest's cadence. Making space for us in this place we all loved.

The darkness became an invitation: to stop, to listen, to feel the parts of these woods we couldn't access when everything was loud and bright. There was nothing to fear, if we embraced it.

We just had to let our eyes adjust.

··········X

“

The darkness became an invitation: to stop, to listen, to feel the parts of these woods we couldn't access when everything was loud and bright.

Carving out a good life

Charlie Gladstone has made a career out of pioneering a new kind of living. Born to a famous name (his great-great grandfather was William Ewart Gladstone, a former prime minister of Great Britain) and heir to two grand properties, he and his wife, Caroline, chose to move away from London and raise their children in the wilds of Scotland. It was there they founded online shop Pedlars, which champions artisan products from around the British Isles.

The Good Life Experience, co-founded with Cerys Matthews and Steve Abbott, is their latest adventure – an annual festival in Wales that's about reconnecting with nature and a community of like-minded people who build things that last, whether that's a relationship, a craft or a meditative practice.

What is The Good Life Experience?

It's a unique celebration of what goes into living 'the good life'. It asks a complex question and tries to simplify it: what do I really want from life? Our answers are presented to our guests over two-and-a-half days each September, and they are: family; amazing food; great music; the ability to learn new crafts and meet new friends; dogs; fascinating talks; engagement with outdoor activities; campfires; nights under canvas; extreme friendliness and politeness; no litter; and the coming together of like-minded people.

What inspired you to start the festival?

I always wanted to do a festival. I was toying with notions of the good life after the global financial meltdown, trying to figure out what it was that people really, truly wanted from their lives. I was asking myself this both because I am a businessman and because I am genuinely interested in the intellectual side of things. I have children, and I wondered if my children really wanted a world of cheap goods, endless shopping, gold-plated restaurants, clothes they could throw away after five wears, endless screen time, food flown to their table from Africa, no spare time. My conclusion was that while these things were perhaps okay in small measures, I wanted them to buy things they treasured and that would last, to know how these things were made, to climb trees and throw axes and discover new ways of looking at the world.

Because I am equal parts brave and reckless, I figured that we might be able to make a festival that celebrates all of this. And because we have a lovely farm in Wales and lots of interesting friends whom we thought might like to perform and suggest people to perform – not to mention two brilliant friends in our co-founders – we gave it a go.

The festival puts a lot of emphasis on connecting with the outdoors and reconnecting with old crafts. Why do you think it's important for people to get outside and use their hands?

I am fundamentally an outdoors person. We raised our six children in the Scottish Highlands, in a remote location, as a conscious choice. We even wrote a book on it, called *The Family Guide to the Great Outdoors*. Everyone should get outside and exhaust themselves from time to time. If all young people got to climb a tree and throw an axe and run up a hill once or twice a week, there would be no fighting in the street. The need to make things with your hands is as old – or older than – the hills. We all have it in us, but mass consumerism has handed it to foreign factories where labour is cheap. But ever since the financial crash in 2008, some people have been thinking about how what they consume is made and what that means, from food to jeans to tableware. These are our people.

"
Everyone should
get outside
and exhaust
themselves from
time to time.

What does the good life mean to the festival founders?

Well, the festival means massive amounts of work, arguments, stress and – simultaneously – fun, pride, creativity, the adrenaline of risk. For me, the good life is all the things we offer at the festival: family, friends both new and old – we have met masses of brilliant new people through the event – music, being outdoors, shenanigans, proper food …

I think of the festival like this: the day is for learning, meeting people, listening, thinking, discovering things, trying new skills and running around; the night is for going a bit bonkers with a great cocktail in your hand and some amazing music.

One of the most popular events at the festival is axe-throwing, which is a very niche skill. What about throwing an axe do you think gives people enjoyment?

The axe is the oldest tool known to humankind. We all have a connection to it, whether we know it or not. And when we hold it and throw it and it hits the target … BOOM!

Do you think people see the festival as a momentary escape from modern life, or more as something they can take home with them?

It's a bit of both. They can come and learn stuff and take those skills home. They can come and have fun and have a monumental hangover on Monday, but feel that they had a life-enhancing experience.

..........x

"

If all young people got to climb a tree and throw an axe and run up a hill once or twice a week, there would be no fighting in the street.

x

The Good Life Festival, held in Wales once a year, is a celebration of life's simple pleasures: stimulating conversation, good music, learning new skills and spending ample amounts of time outside, climbing trees and using your hands.

> **"**
> If there's no next adventure on your mind, then what you're working towards might not be worth the investment.

Choose adventure over email

It can be tempting to forget to look around, captive as we are to the screens in front of us. For Graham Hiemstra, it's the call of adventure that keeps him looking away from his screen in New York City – whether that's hiking the romantically named Rainbow Mountain in Peru or a weekend surf down the coast. He founded The Field, an online adventure repository that entices its readers, through good design and good stories, to look around, to see what's out there, to book that next trip. After all, if you're not exploring … what's the point of it all?

We'd only been on the trail a short while that morning, but our legs still held the memory of miles covered over previous days as we trekked deep into the Peruvian Andes – and let's not even mention the altitude. The four of us crouched down in a semicircle, trying to catch our breaths. With Mount Salkantay looming 6271 metres (20,574 feet) overhead, our Quechua guide performed a healing ceremony. Together, we made cocoa leaf offerings to the spirit protector of the Sacred Valley, who resides in the imposing mountain for which he's named. Like countless others who came before us, as far back as the Inca Empire, we gave thanks and wished each other luck with adventures yet to come. Then we ate some candy bars and starting walking, putting one foot in front of the other.

I grew up in the north-west corner of the United States, where exploring nature was something everyone did. Winters were spent skiing. In summer, my father and I would sleep on the porch under the stars more nights than not. If there was one rule, it was to never waste a clear day inside. I never considered living any other way. Hell, I never even considered living *that* way. It was just how it was. It wasn't until I left that I realised just how influential that early, easy access to adventure was.

These days New York City is home, a third of my time on this rock is gone, and it takes quite a bit more effort to really get outside. Though life in New York isn't easy, it is fun. And surprisingly rewarding, if you're willing to put the work in. At least that's what nearly nine million of us tell ourselves each morning as we cram into subway cars like sardines. But I've come to understand that, for me, the only way to truly thrive here is to leave at every opportunity I get.

Whether it's heading upstate for a weekend of camping, visiting the old growth forests and iconic peaks of America's west coast, or getting truly off the grid in a foreign country, going somewhere new will never get old. Travelling encourages you to expand your worldview and consider alternative perspectives. Nothing puts life's priorities back in place quite like willingly eating mushy food out of a vacuum-packed meal pouch and shitting in a dirt hole you dug yourself. Or, if you prefer a prettier picture, standing atop a 5000-metre (16,400-foot) pass, communing with a mountain spirit.

As a New Yorker, these experiences remind me how unimportant those ever-so-important emails actually are. And that nature is something I need – not a trend or a fad, even if it may feel like that at times.

Regardless of how far-flung or rudimentary the escape, the important thing is to keep them coming. Like all things worth holding on to in life, we require regular maintenance, both mentally and physically, and Mother Nature is the ultimate mechanic. You need to always have an answer to the question 'what's next?' If there's no next adventure on your mind, then what you're working towards might not be worth the investment.

..........x

> "
> Regardless of how far flung or rudimentary the escape, the important thing is to keep them coming.

When Graham Hiemstra headed off into the Peruvian Andes, he knew he would be up for some serious altitude and difficult days. But that was part of what made it a worthy adventure: nothing quite puts life into perspective like having to go it tough for a while.

A van life, captured

....

James Barkman has been living out of a yellow 1976 Volkswagen Westfalia for the last three years, travelling around North America working as an artist and photographer, capturing the lives of itinerant outdoors folk – those who make their living out in nature. The van is his tiny cabin on wheels, and it provides James with everything he needs: bed, sink, wood stove and storage. It lets him live the life he loves.

What inspired you to get a van and start living the van life?

I wanted to live in the woods, shower in the ocean, surf, snowboard and climb, so that's what I did!

The van is my home and only vehicle, so it goes everywhere I go. But generally, I tend to stay near or around the coast and surf as much as possible.

How has living in a van changed the way you live?

I've spent nearly the last three years living on the road, and it has definitely changed my perspective and lifestyle. If you live in a 7.5-square-metre (80-square-foot) box, you'll quickly discover that you can only keep what you absolutely need. My van helps me live in a modest and minimalistic way, and remain undistracted by things that might steal my time and resources.

What sort of challenges does living in a van present?

Depending on where you are, dealing with the weather can be downright brutal. I've spent the last two winters in the Pacific Northwest, and it gets pretty old dealing with constant rain and cold for five months.

How does living in a van fit with your work as a photographer?

I spend a lot of time outdoors for my work, and the van enables me to do just that. I'm also a photographer and have been freelancing for the last while, so I'm able to work according to my needs.

Being active and in the outdoors is a very important part of my life, and is in fact the biggest part of why I made the decision to move into my van full-time. I hope that my work is an honest reflection of my values and interests. I'm very drawn to anything that's vintage, timeless, or has an old-school flair, and the van definitely caters to that aesthetic.

What does van life mean to you?

Van life to me is not a fad or a trend. It's a way to accomplish and pursue the things I love and is a means to an end, not an end in itself.

..........X

"

Van life to me is not a fad
or a trend. It's a way to
accomplish and pursue
the things I love and is a
means to an end, not an
end in itself.

James Barkman lives in his Volkswagen van so he can pursue the life he loves: one where he gets to spend most of his time outside, taking pictures of outdoors folk and being one himself. He focuses his travels in the Pacific Northwest in the United States and never strays far from the ocean.

Cooking in a cold, surreal land

....

Kieran Creevy has made a career out of experiencing the world's tough, wild places – and cooking in them. He was drawn to the Indian side of the Himalayas after hiking the Nepalese side – he'd heard stories that the other side was wilder, more remote. As an expeditionary chef, he searches for those perfect moments of creating food out in nature, that enticing lure of delicious smells rising from a campsite and out over an unfamiliar landscape.

We wake to a gentle rocking. We're floating on a riverboat on a glacial river, surrounded by soaring peaks and some of the most incredible high-altitude landscape we've ever encountered. We're enchanted – mesmerised.

There are lines of pale gold dust in the folds of our clothes, which are stiff with cold. This high in the Himalayas, temperatures are close to freezing, which makes the stove in our riverboat an essential part of our temporary home. Amidst this seemingly desiccated land, hot, fresh river fish arrive on our plates to break our fast; the disparity between the land and its bounty is jarring.

The colours and flow of the rocks in the mountains don't seem real. The whole area has an aura of surrealism about it, as though we've stepped into a Salvador Dalí painting, the endless ripples of valleys and ridges disorienting.

After spending a few days here, it's as though that Dalí painting has suddenly snapped into focus and the scale, the colours, the flow begins to makes sense. Trekking in a landscape this vast is both awe inspiring and contemplative. This is a large part of what has drawn me here before and will probably pull me back again.

Something else is jarring my perception: although we are in the Indian Himalayas, the faces, clothes, language, rituals and food all speak of Tibet.

As is the dinner we have one night: *thukpa* (a Tibetan noodle soup) with spiced bread and pickles. The thukpa is made with hand-rolled noodles: the boat's cook rolls long ribbons of dough on a board, pinching lumps off at random to throw into a pot that is fragrant with spices, herbs and wild greens.

As we sit down to eat, our excitement palpable, darkness and the temperature descend together. The sun plays the losing side against a stark and unforgiving geology, rallying at the last moment with glorious displays of colour. Streaks of rose pink, fuchsia and violet are writ large on these vast canvases of granite, ice and snow.

We revel in the comfort of good company, light, heat, chai and laughter.

..........x

> "
> As we sit down to eat, our excitement palpable, darkness and the temperature descend together ... Streaks of rose pink, fuchsia and violet are writ large on these vast canvases of granite, ice and snow.

Thukpa with wild amaranth and pan-fried river trout

Serves 2

*spice mix (¼ tsp each of ajwain seed, coriander seed, cumin,
    dried curry leaf, fennel seed, fenugreek, mustard seed, nigella
    seed, turmeric)*
2 tbsp oil or 1 tbsp ghee
½ brown onion, diced
4–5 spring onions (scallions), sliced lengthways
1 red chilli, sliced
1 carrot, sliced into ribbons
150–200 g (5–7 oz) fresh udon noodles
500 ml (2 cups) water
pinch dried bonito (tuna) flakes
2 wild trout fillets, boned
sea salt or Himalayan rock salt
large handful purple amaranth
dried seaweed, to garnish
lime zest, to garnish
enough paratha, naan or flatbread to share

Toast the spices in a dry pan. After 1–2 minutes, or when
fragrant, remove from the pan and grind.

Add oil or ghee to the pan and add half the spice mix.
Warm gently to infuse the oils with the spice mix's flavours,
then add the onion. Cook on medium heat until the onion
is translucent.

Heat the water in a kettle while the onion is cooking. Add
the spring onions, chilli, carrot and noodles and sauté gently
for 1 minute. Add the boiling water and a few bonito flakes
and simmer for 5 minutes. Taste and season if needed.

Heat a little oil in a separate pan over medium heat. When
the oil is hot, place the trout fillets in the pan and cook
until the flesh has just turned from translucent to opaque in
the centre.

Ladle the soup into bowls, add the amaranth and top with the
trout. Sprinkle with dried seaweed, lime zest and sea salt.

Serve with some warm paratha, naan or other flatbread.

The Himalayas have long drawn dreamers and adventurers with their dramatic beauty, challenging slopes and peaks that seem to touch the sky. Sunsets like this one in the Sangla Valley in Himachal Pradesh, India, are what expedition chef Kieran Creevy says 'has drawn me here before, and will probably pull me back again'.

The weight of the stars

In the city, you'll be lucky to see more than a smattering of stars in the night sky, and even then you might actually be looking at a satellite or plane. While Lauren Whybrow has always looked up at the night sky, it took a trip into deep country to reveal what had been obscured behind the city pollution – a universe hanging heavy with stars.

She laughed when I suggested we bring a lantern outside and told me that I wouldn't need the extra light. We stepped off the porch and walked towards the gate that separated the house from the property; struggling in the fading light cast off by the porch, I lifted up the latch, pushed open the gate, and then we were outside. There were no lights except for the house at our backs and a universe of stars in front of us.

It was my first night in this part of the country. I was staying on a friend's farm about seven hours' drive north of Sydney, Australia. Her property was the only family-owned farm left in the valley, a warm weatherboard house with a protective army of sheep and cattle. It was surrounded by land that belonged to banks and insurance companies, building up wealth to pass on to investors.

During the day, the conviviality of her family, the clutter of a working farm and the calls of the animals made me feel comfortable, though the territory was strange to my city-raised self. But at night, when I stepped away from the house, the valley suddenly felt vast and unpeopled – the land foreign, the stars unknown.

As we inched our way farther and farther from the house, feeling for rocks and listening for snakes, the light behind us dimmed and the sky in front of us grew. Planets and stars and space junk filled the sky, streaking across it. There was the Southern Cross; there was the constellation known locally as The Saucepan; there was the Milky Way, its outline clear and faintly purple.

The universe seemed close to us, bowing in under its own weight. Lights I had never seen before, and had no chance of remembering, clustered in my eyes. This was the sky that had guided early explorers, the beginnings of humanity. It was ancient and new, strange and familiar. We have lost that skill, that ability to be guided by the stars. Instead the universe feels cold, uncaring, callous in its unfathomable size. But instead of feeling small, I started to find my place, somewhere between the constellations and the moon. I knew that sky didn't care that I looked up, that we looked up. And yet it guided us all the same, markers of our place on Earth, in the universe.

I turned and turned and turned, trying to take in the whole sky at once. My friend stood next to me, silent and smiling. It was familiar to her, this sky cleared of pollution and the lights of the city. It would never be familiar to me. But now that I am home, back in the city, I still stare at the sky, trying to find a glimpse of that weight through the clouds and smog and blinking planes. It can't guide me here, blocked by the lights of the city. But sometimes, just sometimes, I think I see it.
..........X

"

This was the sky that had guided early explorers, the beginnings of humanity. It was ancient and new, strange and familiar.

Follow your feet

Growing up, Max Blackmore's parents often took him out camping and hiking in the hills and along the Australian coastline. Like any child, he didn't always enjoy these family outings. But after the halcyon days of his early twenties and being desk-bound in his career as a graphic designer, Max rediscovered hiking and his connection with the outdoors.

He did research to try and find places to visit, beautiful spots in nature with accessible hikes, but he discovered that there was little information out there for people who wanted inspiration and not a step-by-step walking guide cluttered with latitudes and longitudes, 'turn left, then turn right'. So he founded Left Foot Right Foot, an online hiking guide that tells you about each walk and offers helpful information, but lets you discover the rest for yourself; through it, he's found a community of like-minded hikers and adventurers.

What inspired Left Foot Right Foot?

I always hiked as a kid, and then I discovered it again in my twenties. A few friends were hiking, too, and we'd go out on overnight hikes. I've always loved Wilsons Prom National Park on the southern coast of Australia. Most birthdays I'd go there and generally end up at the lighthouse, just realising how beautiful it was. The first walk I put on the site was in Wilsons Prom.

I was travelling around the east coast of Australia a few years ago and you could only find free maps, all of which had tourist parks, caravan parks, adventure parks – all the stuff I wanted to stay away from. They would have a big green square that said 'national park', but no information about it. And then when you look at the physical books on bushwalking it's information overload.

Walking is basically easy and doesn't require that much setup or gear. I guess that was one of the core points of the site: to show people how accessible hiking is. You don't need a lot of bells and whistles, just a tent that's not ridiculously heavy. Just get out there.

Do you have a community on the site now?

There's a community in our contributors, because we've got thirty-plus people who have contributed to the site. It's exactly what I wanted, which is for people to build a community themselves and just be able to explore each other's photography and connect with other people going for hikes … an appreciation of places you haven't been, tips, that sort of stuff.

Is Wilsons Prom still your favourite place to hike?

In Victoria, I'd definitely say Wilsons Prom is my favourite. I could go there for the rest of my life. There's this one beach, Little Waterloo Bay, that's just straight out of the movie *The Beach*, it's like no one's ever been there. If you go to the park in winter it's even better, because if you walk through the campsites they are overrun with animals like potteroos and wallabies.

What do you like about hiking?

There are two types of hiking. When you do it on your own you get time to think and take photos, and just be in nature, which I think is the best part: just being surrounded by it. Even if you go to the same place every week, you'll see something different, you'll experience something different. It's always changing.

And then with people it's the same – you get to be with people experiencing the same thing. It's when you get to a spot, you camp, and that waking-up point or that going-to-bed point is just perfect. You've had that sunset that's perfect and the temperature's perfect, and then you wake up and it's the same. Or when you're trying to light a fire. It's a feeling of being content. You can't really explain it.

……….X

Avid hiker Max Blackwell could limit himself to exploring Wilsons Promontory National Park in Victoria, Australia, for the rest of his life and be content. This park off Australia's wild southern coast captures everything he loves about hiking: beautiful beaches, plentiful wildlife and epic views like this one from the top of Mount Oberon.

Sharing coffee and connection

Erik Gordon didn't try his first cup of coffee until he was twenty-two years old and partway through a bike journey across America. It wasn't a big decision: he was cold and the coffee was warm. But when Erik took his first sip, he was floored. Suddenly he could see why communities gather and connect over this simple brew. He decided that this was what he was meant to be doing: making coffee and creating connections with America's outdoor community of climbers, hikers and riders – a bunch of people who also live life doing the things they love. So Erik bought a Volkswagen van and started Carabiner Coffee. He now travels the country in it, selling good coffee, good coffee beans and living his version of the good life.

There is no greater accomplishment than living a journey that is totally and completely yours. For me, that means travelling the country in an old VW van called Ol' Blue, spreading love through simple cups of coffee. Coffee has the power to bring people together, and it's my mission to use that connection to inspire people to take a chance and believe in the dream that keeps them up at night.

When I had my first cup of coffee, I was a dirtbag climber in search of the life of adventure I had always wanted. I drank a cup of coffee to keep warm on a cold coastal day, and it opened my eyes to new possibilities. From then on, travel and coffee and living a free life were connected in a way that I couldn't seem to shake.

A few years later, after moving to Colorado, I started to learn the coffee trade inside and out. I soon gained enough knowledge and confidence to set out on my own coffee journey. I knew it also needed to be focused on nature and experiencing wild places.

I found Ol' Blue through an online listing a few states away. After a couple of months of talking with the seller, I made my final offer without ever having driven or seen the van in person. Over the following months, I turned it into a home and a coffee shop on wheels.

When I finally drove Ol' Blue out of town and over a freezing mountain pass, toes numb and fingers white, I couldn't help but smile. I'd put myself into a position where I had no other option but to embrace the journey. You always hear people talking about wanting to live a life with no maps or limits, and this was it. This was my chance. This was my dream.

Some days the van breaks down and I don't make it to where I'm going. But I still find myself smiling. I'm here, I'm alive and I'm spending my days exactly the way they were meant to be spent, spreading love the best way I know how – through a damn good cup of coffee.

..........x

"

You always hear people talking about wanting to live a life with no maps or limits, and this was it. This was my chance. This was my dream.

Erik Gordon bought a van, converted it into a coffee shop/home on wheels, and hit the road to epic adventure. He drives around the West Coast of the United States, selling coffee to other outdoors folk who like making new friends over a cup of joe.

The meaning of travel

Matty Hannon quit his job working in advertising to ride a motorcycle from Alaska to Argentina, surfing the waves and the road all 13,500 kilometres (8500 miles) down the long trans-American coastline. He didn't go in pursuit of that life-changing moment, that picture-perfect revelation, but instead with the plan to find and document inspiring people across America with his camera. It was a trip characterised by curiosity and a deep appreciation for the people and lands he met along the way. This curiosity led to a chance encounter with a girl named Heather (see page 188), who ended up joining Matty on the road.

Leaving home is an exhilarating prospect: the allure of an open road, the promise of rolling waves, of neatly groomed ski hills with perfect fireside retreats. It's easy to let your imagination run wild at the sight of the magazines in the supermarket's travel section, while your tired fingers grip the sticky handles of your coffee-laden shopping trolley.

You gaze at the glossy covers. How good would life be if you could just make *that* your next destination? Make those smiling people your friends? Have just one of those '15 Vacations That Will Change Your Life'?

But beyond the allure of a few weeks off work, some stimulating views, a peer-approved tan and extra fodder for your Instagram – is all this travel really growing you? Is it benefiting us? Is it promoting understanding and tolerance, or just fostering elitism and homogeny? Are we learning from the places we visit, or are we imposing ourselves on places that would be better off without us? Aren't we supposed to be using less energy, staying local, buying local? And why aren't we returning from these 'life-changing' destinations with … different lives?

Perhaps because like most marketing, social media and all things shiny, it lacks a little soul or deeper meaning – travel, for many, has become just another commodity. But the real essence of travel is still there for discovery … it just helps to have a meaningful reason to go.

In my own travels, I chose to make film my medium, surfing my canvas, and time my currency. I quit my job in Australia and embarked on a trans-continental motorcycle and surfing journey from Alaska to Argentinean Patagonia. I aimed to find and interview inspiring people across the Americas, to document their ideas. One of the first sequences I filmed was an urban farm in British Columbia, where I interviewed

> " Travel, for many, has become just another commodity. But the real essence of travel is still there for discovery … it just helps to have a meaningful reason to go.

When Matty Hannon hit the road on his motorcycle, heading south from Alaska towards Argentina, he didn't expect some of what he found along the way: fascinating people to interview, new ways of thinking and a girl with whom to fall in love and sleep under stars in the Atacama Desert.

its owner. That cute entrepreneur ended up joining me on my journey to South America. Heather and I have been together ever since.

We rode south, interviewing fifty people across North and South America. It was in those deep conversations that I found meaning in the idea of 'travel' or 'adventure', immersing myself in diverse opinions, reflecting and making adjustments in the way I chose to live. Our interviews with farmers living in a traditional farming community in the Andes, who inspired us to sell our motorcycles and continue our journey on horseback.

It's at such times that I find documentary filmmaking a beautiful process. By offering someone a microphone and a willing ear, you're offering them the chance to be heard. And in contrast to the surface conversations that define most people's days, you can ask deep and probing questions and be met with honest, sometimes profound, responses that have the power to rattle even your core beliefs.

But just like you don't need a glossy magazine travel holiday – not really – most people don't need a documentary camera and a microphone to experience the world. The only true necessity is deep appreciation and curiosity. Perhaps we need that now more than ever.

That alone behoves us to travel – just where and how *well* we travel is up to us.

..........X

"

... most people don't need a documentary camera and a microphone to experience the world. The only true necessity is deep appreciation and curiosity.

"

... I found meaning
in the idea of 'travel'
or 'adventure',
immersing myself
in diverse opinions,
reflecting and making
adjustments in the way
I chose to live.

"

Capturing the beauty of a damaged world

Brooke Holm became a photographer almost by accident. She was working in an advertising agency when someone put a camera in her hand and told her to go take photos of some outdoor billboards the company had produced. She took the photos, everyone was pleased, and Brooke was hooked, so much so that she went back to school to develop her skills. Brooke has become a sought-after commercial photographer in Australia and the United States, but it's her work photographing nature – the human-made and human-affected places of the world – that truly speak to and for her. They showcase her passion for the environment and for highlighting places many of us don't get to see.

You mix a commercial practice with your own artistic work. How do you balance the two?

While my commercial work is driven by living and working in a big city amongst the craziness, my personal, artistic work is the complete opposite. It's my escape and my chance to shoot exactly what I want. There is no brief or client to please – it's all about what is important to me. Currently, this work is exploring a deeper understanding of the world in a social and environmental sense.

My art has always been driven by landscapes, and humans' relationships to nature, particularly mine. However, these days I feel there are deeper avenues to explore – ones that might not be pleasant, but that contain vital stories and important questions.

How important is nature to your work?

Nature is the most important aspect of my work. My practice is centred around the environment and our relationship with it. Nature and humans affect each other in many ways, so there should be a mutual give and take. Instead it seems one-sided, where we take and hardly give anything back. I'm constantly wrestling with ideas about how to convey the importance of respecting and nurturing our planet. Our dependency on its resources has become such a big burden, in a very unsustainable way.

Everything in this world is connected. That reality becomes more alarming as our seas become more acidic and species die out, which is leading to some devastating consequences – all because of us. We can't fight a volcano with weapons, and we definitely can't buy a new Great Barrier Reef once we eventually destroy it.

What does nature mean to you personally?

It's the only thing that really makes perfect sense to me. I don't know for sure, but I feel it's partly based on a primal instinct where the connection is naturally strong and unexplainable.

When I see all the terrible things affecting our environment, it really disturbs me. There is a deep desire in me for exploration and discovery, for finding new perspectives on places in both a physical and mental sense. Nature finds a way to make you question what really matters. Finding these landscapes and documenting them is a very personal thing, but I feel a responsibility to share my findings with people, as many are not fortunate enough to leave their hometown or do not remember how to look outside their comfort zone. I like to inspire deeper thought and make someone feel something.

Last year you produced spectacular photos of Shark Bay in Western Australia. These works speak powerfully of the landscape's strong colours and stark land. What drew you to Shark Bay?

Shark Bay is part of a UNESCO World Heritage Site, so its flora and fauna are protected. But amongst this natural landscape is a salt mine (pictured at bottom right), not part of the heritage site, where salt is harvested and exported for human consumption and for use in chemical products.

My project 'Salt and Sky' explores the ways in which humans can physically change the physical appearance of the land. It's a very good example of us taking from the environment. The ponds have gone through a number of expansions, which can lead to the displacement of marine life.

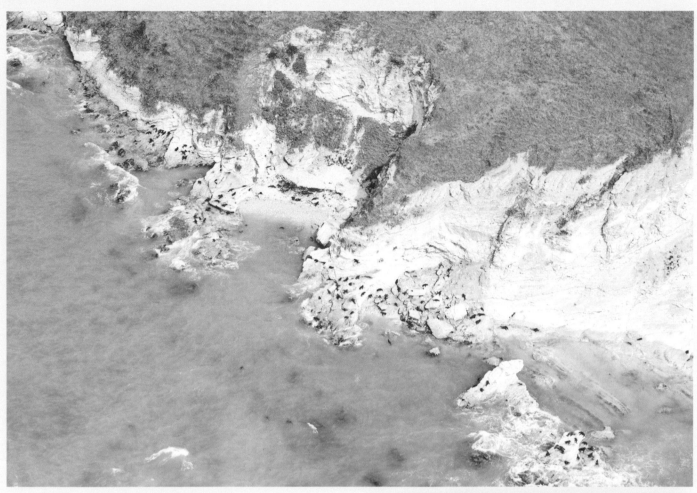

"

Nature finds a way to
make you question
what really matters.

> "
> We can't fight a
> volcano with weapons,
> and we definitely
> can't buy a new Great
> Barrier Reef once we
> eventually destroy it.

"

This archipelago stands in isolation from the rest of the world, but it also stands for what we will lose if we are not educated and willing to act.

"

So while viewing aerial images of this aesthetically beautiful human-made place, it's also important to note the sacrifices that were made for it to exist.

Do you constantly challenge yourself to think of new angles and new approaches?

Absolutely. The way I see things and photograph them is very intuitive, so the physical act of shooting comes naturally. I know straight away when I have a shot and when I don't, and there is always an interplay of angles, perspectives, shape, colour, pattern and light. I constantly challenge myself to push the limits, do my research and find places to travel that spark my intrigue and speak to my concerns and desires.

Before the Shark Bay photos, you took a photographic series of the Arctic. What was it like travelling to the cold, far reaches of the world?

My Arctic expedition is something I will never forget. I travelled to Svalbard, an isolated island north of Norway, by myself, where I met a small expedition crew of twelve people. We spent ten days together on the rocking Arctic Ocean, travelling in and out of fjords, breaking through sea ice, witnessing the magnitude of the glaciers and studying polar bears and other wildlife. I stood on the bow of the ship, where at one point I became the northernmost person in the world. Up there, you really get a perspective shift.

The Arctic is constantly in the news as being the place where climate change is most noticeable. Did you find that when you were there? Did you try and capture that with your work?

It is more starkly noticeable, yes. The Arctic warms at least twice as fast as the rest of the world; polar bear numbers are dwindling because the amount of sea ice melting increases each year. They are dependent on the sea ice – they cannot hunt or eat without it, and so many of them end up starving each summer. The glaciers have retreated at alarming rates and the melting permafrost is causing potent methane gases to escape into the atmosphere.

My Arctic series depicts an otherworldly landscape that is in danger of destruction. It's not a place many will see in their lifetime, so I went there to shine light on it by documenting its current state, raising awareness of the imminent threat to its existence.

What do you hope people see when they look at those photos?

I hope they recognise how special the Arctic is. It is such a beautiful, dangerously fragile environment, but it's difficult to enact change if you don't have an appreciation for something. Especially when it's so far away from most people (out of sight, out of mind). This archipelago stands in isolation from the rest of the world, but it also stands for what we will lose if we are not educated and willing to act. My hope is to inspire a growing awareness, at the very least.

You've been to some incredibly diverse places for your artistic practice. How do you choose and plan each location?

It has happened organically so far. I get an idea in my head and I pursue it. Svalbard was always on my list because I remember it appearing in Philip Pullman's novel *Northern Lights*, which I read when I was younger. Other trips have been sparked by pictures I have seen or articles I have read. We are fortunate to have access to imagery of all kinds of places, so I can scope it out before I go.

So … where to next?

Most likely Greenland, in order to continue my Svalbard and Iceland work. Otherwise, there is a giant list that I just have to tackle one at a time.

..........x

Though photographer Brooke Holm is disturbed by the effects of human action on the natural world, she finds the act of capturing places like Canada a way of shining much needed light on the connection between us and the world we live in – that we are connected, whether it feels that way or not.

The lost art of crossing mountains

Daniel Wakefield Pasley co-founded *Yonder Journal*, an American outdoor magazine that doesn't just talk about adventure in nature, but also studies it, pokes it, prods it, looks at it from all angles and sometimes, just sometimes, attempts to conquer it. Yes, the team behind *Yonder Journal* likes to do things a bit … differently. That includes setting themselves awe-inspiring and jaw-clenching challenges, like their project Dead Reckoning – an attempt to ride lightweight bicycles across the world's untamed mountain passes in a high-altitude, high-flying series of adventures. Mountains are monumental barriers – but sometimes, in order to evolve and grow and all of those things, you need to dare to cross one or two.

Mountains, historically and culturally speaking, have been one of humankind's biggest and most interesting obstacles when it comes to travel and trade. They're topographically awesome. They're literally and metaphorically breathtaking. And, most importantly, they are fearsome and hazardous, and to tempt their transit can invite dire consequences.

Crossing mountains is in our nature. We are driven to push boundaries, make discoveries and know the unknowable. In other words, we're a risk-taking lot. And as any pioneer – George Donner, Hannibal, Sir Edmund Hillary, Napoleon Bonaparte – could tell you, there is ~~always~~ probably something good on the other side of a mountain: a new language, better cheese, curious musical instruments, gold, rainbows, golden rainbows, etc. But only if you make it over. So please make it over. In the spirit of making it over …

In 2015 the team behind *Yonder Journal* set out to investigate, document and publish the lost art of Over-Mountain Exploration (O-ME) in an era when people are more interested in climbing mountains than going over them. We called this project Dead Reckoning. For two years we applied the technologies and methodologies of adventure-cycling, bike-packing, and ultra-lightweight touring to multi-day expeditions with a focus on crossing mountains using a variety of trade routes, both ancient and modern. Our investigation of these trade routes took us to New Zealand, Bolivia, Canada, the United States, Australia, Colombia and the Republic of Georgia.

Why a bicycle? Why not a donkey, a motorcycle, a helicopter, a sail boat or simply a pair of hiking boots? Because bicycles are the most pragmatic, useful and efficient means of personal transportation ever invented. They cover ground at the perfect speed, are dependable, simple, adaptable and packable. You have to feed a donkey, put gas in a motorcycle, do so many things to a helicopter. Hiking is so slow. And anyway, have you ever tried sailing a boat over a mountain? Still unconvinced? Think about this: bicycles use the wheel, which is second only to fire in the list of best inventions ever. And we all know fire shouldn't really count.

So was it worth it? Let's see …

1) Did we discover new cheese flavours and exotic fruits? (Yes, but most of them were gross and flavourless. Colombia has the best fruits in the world. That's not hyperbole: it's science. Just ask for a *jugo con leche*.)

> **"**
>
> Crossing mountains is in our nature. We are driven to push boundaries, make discoveries and know the unknowable. In other words, we're a risk-taking lot.

2) Did we really need that yellow fever vaccination? (Probably. We didn't contract yellow fever so, yeah, probably. But we also spent most of our time above 4500 metres [15,000 feet]. Not even yellow fever can survive that kind of elevation.)

3) How much did the helicopter ride in those southern alps cost, anyway? ($1750 USD.)

4) What does it mean to 'work a grizz'? (It's a long story, but can be summed up this way: stare at it, yell at it, back away, but don't back down. Also, shit your pants.)

5) Can it really snow in the middle of North American summer over and over and over and over again? (Yup.)

6) Does altitude sickness mirror or cause – or cause and then mirror – a panic attack? (Double yup. Bonus: extreme altitude also gives you very strange dreams.)

..........x

"

... there is ~~always~~ probably something good on the other side of a mountain: a new language, better cheese, curious musical instruments, gold, rainbows, golden rainbows, etc. But only if you make it over.

Daniel Wakefield Pasley and the team at adventure mag *Yonder Journal* believe that there's always something good to be found on the other side of a mountain. For their project Dead Reckoning, they biked across mountains all over the world just to see what they might find there.

The power of everyday adventures

Alastair Humphreys has never shied away from adventure – in fact, he's made a point of embracing it. By eight, he was running across mountains in races like the Yorkshire 3 Peaks. By fourteen, he was cycling off-road across England. During university, he cycled long routes from Pakistan to India, Turkey to Italy, and beyond. After he graduated, he threw himself wholeheartedly into the chase for adventure, cycling over continents, rowing across oceans and hiking through the wild places of the world.

Though he's gone on some epically big adventures, Alastair believes in the power of going small – embracing the adventures waiting for us just outside our own front doors. He calls these trips microadventures: small, cheap, local journeys that anyone can fit in around their daily commutes and commitments. The idea is to find everyday ways to rediscover the joy of being outside, discovering new things and spending a night out under the open sky. To see adventure not as a list of far-flung locations and daring deeds, but as an attitude.

You started adventuring right out of university, cycling around the world, rowing across the Atlantic and walking the length of a sacred river in India, among others. What draws you to adventure?

I like exciting, unusual things. If they are spiced with risk, then so much the better. I'm no daredevil or adrenaline junkie, but I relish activities that scare me a little and call for enterprise and enthusiasm. A call to adventure.

If I go somewhere I have never been, step out of my comfort zone and have little idea what tomorrow will bring, then I know I am going to have an adventure. When normal life starts to feel a little bit, well, normal, an adventure is called for.

> "
> In my opinion, adventure is mainly in the mind. Adventure is an attitude.

Life's not all work, seriousness and planning for pensions. 'I won't have it,' declared writer Annie Dillard. 'The world is wilder than that in all directions, more dangerous and bitter, more extravagant and bright. We are making hay when we should be making whoopee.' In other words, there is a time for simple fun.

Adventure in the form of travel is what many people dream of doing when they retire or win the lottery. I chose not to wait for retirement or a windfall, and I didn't let a lack of money stop me; I just worked out how to travel cheaply. In order to take long trips overseas, I learnt how to sleep wild, saving on accommodation costs. I walked so that transportation cost nothing. I ate the cheapest food. My walk across India cost just 500 pounds, of which 300 pounds was the plane ticket.

I travel, amongst everything else, to seek out fun and the warm glow of the sun on my face (though come noon, I will be sweating and cursing it). I slurp mangoes and join in village cricket matches. It is a lot of fun. When people ask, 'Why do you travel?' there's no simpler and more honest answer than that.

For you, what makes something an adventure?

Most people would agree that cycling across one of the world's great mountain ranges is an adventure. So is waking in a tent buried in snow, or paddling whitewater rapids, or rowing through a tropical storm through steep waves lit by a silver moon. But adventure need not be any of these things. I think the core of adventure is actually something much deeper, though it is undoubtedly expressed though travel, expeditions and extreme sports.

The best way to define adventure is to think, briefly, about what adventure is *not*. It is not about world records, beating others, making a story, a film, a pile of cash, getting famous online, generating 'content', or repeating what you've already done, but faster.

In my opinion, adventure is mainly in the mind. Adventure is an attitude. It's doing something that is new; something difficult, exciting, daunting. Something with a significant chance of failure and an enticing sense of satisfaction upon completion. Adventure involves unpredictability and uncertainty – that's part of the ultimate reward.

It should be pursued with determination, significant effort, curiosity and (when possible) a sense of humour.

Even though you've experienced some epic adventures in far-flung places, you've also championed the idea of adventures close to home. Can you explain what a microadventure is, and why/how you came up with the idea?

As I toured around, giving speeches about my adventures and the joy of getting out and having them, I kept hearing the same thing over and over: 'You are an Adventurer. I am a Normal Person.' Which, to me, is total rubbish. Everyone is both an adventurer and a normal person – myself included. I wanted to show that the only barrier between the two is the one we build ourselves; I wanted to bring that barrier down by helping people find adventure in whatever form they could. So I decided to dedicate a year to discovering my own country by going small – really small. I went in search of tiny adventures close to home.

Most people don't have time to cycle around the world or the level of fitness needed to climb Everest, but that doesn't mean they can't go on adventures. So microadventures are deliberately small in scale. They are short, cheap, simple and often local. But they also tax the adventurer, both mentally and physically. They push me to discover new places and escape everyday routine, even if only briefly.

Maybe you're feeling like the city you live in is boring or stifling, and that somewhere wild is where adventure exists. Maybe you liked camping as a child, but now your obligations keep you from getting out. It's these very feelings that microadventures are meant to break through. They are meant to grab you, firmly but politely, and shake you into rediscovering rivers and mountains, to remember the many joys to be found in exploring the world around you.

Part of the crux of microadventures is that people can go and do something new anywhere, anytime – including the hours after and before work. Is this just about ease and accessibility, or do you think there's something special about seeing your home with new eyes?

Both! It's about looking differently at your circumstances (lack of time) or your home (finding adventure in familiar places). Once you learn that you can find wildness and adventure close to home, you have fewer excuses to blame inertia on a lack of time or resources.

" I relish activities that scare me a little and call for enterprise and enthusiasm. A call to adventure.

What are some of the microadventures you've done?

I walked a lap of the 190-kilometre (118-mile)-long M25 highway that circles London, which was far from the best night's sleep I've ever had (the highway never sleeps). I also went on the same overnight hike in the same woods, but across all four seasons so I could get to know it in all its forms.

I even grabbed a bivvy bag, Thermarest, raincoat and my camera and went for a microadventure around my home. I wanted to make the radius big enough that I could leave at five in the afternoon, complete the circle and be back at my desk by nine the next morning. It was cheap, logistically simple and an excellent way to explore and discover my local wild places, and much more slowly than I normally do. It reminded me how easy it is to get away from ugly, built-up areas and find tiny pockets of beautiful wilderness. All you have to do is take the time to look.

Microadventures can be really flexible based on time and location – do you have an absolute rule for what makes a microadventure?

Douglas Bader once said, 'Rules are for the guidance of wise men, and the obedience of fools …' I don't mind what people do, so long as they do *something*. Having said that, I believe that spending a night out under the stars makes an experience significantly more memorable, rewarding and potentially transformative than just having a day trip. By all means, ride your bike all day. But if you sleep out in a bivvy bag, too, you will have done something far more adventurous.

You became National Geographic's Adventurer of the Year in 2012 because of your work on microadventures. Why do you think this idea resonated with people?

I believe it was because it was accessible, achievable and realistic for normal people with busy, real lives. A lot of the adventures we consume are vicarious – almost like adventure-porn. Cycling around the world, rowing the Atlantic: it's titillating, exciting, but not anything someone with a job and a family will ever do. Microadventures have struck a chord because they have brought adventure to ordinary people, rather than making them feel left out and inferior.

What would you say to someone who says they can't get out on an adventure?

I would say that you can.

I'm aware, of course, that some people genuinely have significant hurdles in life – disability, for example – but for the vast majority of the world, this is what I would tell them: instead of saying to yourself, 'I don't have the time to do this' or 'I can't afford to go on that trip', try saying the same thing, but with 'choose *not* to'. 'I *choose not* to do this.' 'I *choose not* to save up for that trip.' Because most of the time, if you want something – really want it – you can find a way.

Saying to yourself that you *choose not* to do it might help clear your head and make you realise that what you thought was a genuine constraint is actually just a mental block you have created for yourself.

Perhaps you are scared; perhaps it will be really difficult; perhaps you don't quite have the will to make it happen. But at least now you'll be a little closer to having an honest answer.

How do you balance microadventures with bigger adventures?

Microadventures fit nicely into the gaps between big ones – no balance required. I try to have as many of both kinds as I can! And in the periods between big ones, when I'm writing/saving/busy with everyday life, I escape as often as I can for a night on a hill in a bivvy bag.

··········X

The Northern Lights may look paler than you imagined they would. But if you are far from city lights and you let your eyes adjust to the darkness, an aurora is an incredible, mesmerising sight. The shimmering, dancing movements of an aurora are nothing short of miraculous.

Chasing the lights

We huddled down in our tent in Jasper National Park in British Columbia, Canada, trying to keep warm against the summer mountain cold. My fiancé and I had spent the past two months living out of car and tent, hiking our way around North America's mountainous parks. It had been a bad summer for wildfires, the smoke coating Jasper's skies with a sickly haze. But when we'd gone to bed, stars were appearing. All was clear, crisp and so cold I couldn't feel my hands.

I was tired and wanting sleep, but the guys camping next to us were talking late and loud around their campfire.

'It's the Northern Lights', one of them said. At least that's what I thought he said.

It's not the right time of year for the lights, said my annoyed, half-asleep, want-to-stay-asleep brain. *It's too cold to get up, anyway.*

But we did, because we had to check. And there they were: green, snaking rivers that moved so fast they were hard to make sense of. They stuttered and flickered like stop-motion animation, changing shape between our blinks. Blink once and they cut across the dark in those winding rivers; blink again and they were bright glass curtains, hanging like icicles from the edge of a roof. We never saw the moment when they changed from river to curtain – they just were, and then were not. They weren't as bright a green as in photos I'd seen of them – cameras pick up and amplify colour in ways the human eye can't – but they were still clearly visible, glowing close. They filled the sky, but felt illusory: everywhere and nowhere, too big for the mind to hold.

It felt like there should be some noise to go with it, but the whole show went on in silence. The only sound was the shallow huff of our breaths.

The lights are called the *Aurora Borealis* in the northern hemisphere – named after the Roman goddess of the dawn (Aurora) and the Greek name for the north wind (Borea) – and *Aurora Australis* in the southern hemisphere.

People have gleaned meaning from them for as long as they have appeared: as omens of war and plague, old memories and new beginnings. Some have seen them as animals hunted and killed; the ghosts of hunters; children lost at birth. Others have seen them as gods, giants and battling dragons. Signs of clash and friction, which isn't far from what they are: collisions between the charged particles of Sun and Earth.

The Sun's turbulent surface sometimes throws off particles that make their way towards Earth. While Earth's magnetic field is usually able to repel them, sometimes they slip through and are drawn to our planet's magnetic poles, where they collide with atoms in our atmosphere and create a chemical reaction that we see as light. The colours of an aurora depend on altitude and what types of atoms are colliding – greens and reds for oxygen; blue and purple-reds for nitrogen.

You'll find them close to the poles, in places like Canada and Greenland, Australia and New Zealand. Wherever you find them, they are like nothing else you'll ever see.

We watched them for however long they lasted, necks craned and eyes wide. It could have been ten minutes or an hour. The lights cast a spell on us that made us forget to check our watches, afraid that we would miss the moment when they started to fade. I dug through my memory for the chemical explanation for them, but right then they didn't feel like something to be explained or measured. They were wild and unknowable, made beautiful because you know they won't last.

..........X

Words by Kate Armstrong, a writer, editor, teacher and lover of living in tents. Images and captions by Ben Leshchinsky, a civil engineer and self-taught photographer who loves capturing the skies around his home in America's Pacific Northwest.

You might not realise it, but when you watch a video of an aurora you are not watching the natural phenomenon in real time. The videos are actually time-lapse videos with many long-exposure photos as frames. To capture the phenomenon, you typically need to use a tripod and keep the camera's shutter (the thing that goes 'click') open for at least a few seconds to gather the light, which is often fainter than expected.

You don't need a fancy camera to capture an aurora. You just need a tripod, your DSLR and the widest-angle lens possible. Set the lens focus to manual and focus on infinity, ensuring faraway objects appear in focus. Make sure the lens is set at the widest possible aperture (the smaller the 'f' number, the better). Set the camera's light sensitivity, or ISO, to anywhere from 800 to 3200 and the shutter speed anywhere from 10 to 30 seconds. Using the camera's timer or a shutter release remote, aim the lens at the aurora, click the shutter and wait; even the dimmest aurora becomes vibrant.

The tradition of stone and steam

Growing tired of the capitalist crush and relentless rush of London, artists Holly Gable and Angus Fulton left the city for life on the road, travelling slowly through Europe, then Asia, then back again. They don't live in isolation, but instead experience different cultures, communities and ways of living through work exchange programs. After a few years on the road, Holly and Angus found themselves in Finland, helping prepare a house for winter. They spent a lot of time in the sauna, where they discovered that no connection is stronger than one created in this world of heat and sweat.

There is a Finnish saying: All men are created equal; but nowhere more so than in a sauna.

Naked, climbing up onto a bench. We can vaguely make out the shape of other people in the small, dark room. The smell of hot wood almost scalds our nostrils. We slowly lower ourselves into the heat, skin pressed against the steady, warm wood; it's grounding, holding us. We melt.

Fire crackles. On top of the wood-burning stove is a pile of rocks. Someone dunks a ladle-like scoop into a bucket of water and throws it over them. The water evaporates immediately, sizzling loud. It marks the coming of a wave of hot steam that envelops us from feet to face. We melt some more.

A sauna is a place of softening, calm contemplation and gently spoken words. A sacred space. The act of throwing water to the stones to create the steam cloud is called *löyly* (pronounced LEWle). An ancient word that means 'spirit of life', löyly is a celebration of the elements: fire in the sauna stove, earth in the rocks, water thrown upon them and transformed into air.

After long days restoring Micke and Jouni's old wooden house in southern Finland, time in the sauna was a reward for our bodies and minds. We were preparing the house for winter: climbing it with nail guns, fixing on wooden cladding, painting it with home-cooked linseed oil and building window frames.

Out of the heat, we run down the jetty and into the lake. Time stops in that moment before the panic, before the plunge, with just enough air to breathe. Hot skin meets cold surface in an electric, whole-body rush. As we emerge, eyes and ears at water level, it starts pouring with rain. We can see, hear, taste, feel, smell nothing but the dense rush of plummeting rain droplets hitting the surface of the lake and sending splashes high above our heads. All-encompassing, exhilarating and hilarious. The rain stops and we float around, naked, in the misty silence.

"

We slowly lower ourselves into the heat, skin pressed against the steady, warm wood; it's grounding, holding us. We melt.

> **"**
> We were submerged in euphoria; partly because of the sauna-swim-sauna endorphin rush, but mostly because of what we had discovered ...

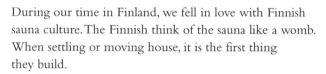

"

A sauna is a place of softening, calm contemplation and gently spoken words. A sacred space.

During our time in Finland, we fell in love with Finnish sauna culture. The Finnish think of the sauna like a womb. When settling or moving house, it is the first thing they build.

Dark and meditative, the sauna is a space free of hierarchies in which one should not discuss title or religion. It is a practical place where water is heated for washing, where rye is dried, where meat is cured and malt is prepared. A space for physical and mental cleansing, the soothing of tense muscles and minds. A place to sit together in quiet celebration of our interdependent existence with nature.

When further adventures in Estonia beckoned and the time came for us to say goodbye to our Finnish family, we took a trip to a Helsinki smoke sauna. Cooling off from the heat in the lake, up to our cheeks in the icy September water, we peered at the sun setting through the orange and yellow leaves of autumnal aspen and birch.

We were submerged in euphoria; partly because of the sauna-swim-sauna endorphin rush, but mostly because of what we had discovered: the profound happiness that comes from helping and sharing, and that love, friendship and kindness can be found everywhere.

..........X

Travelling the world on trade

Before starting Pixel Trade, Shantanu Starick was working as a photographer and studying architecture in Australia, travelling overseas one or two times a year. He started Pixel Trade as an experiment to see how long and how far he could travel the world without spending any money, trading his skills as a photographer for bed and board.

The rules of the trade were simple: in exchange for him photographing your project, you would help him travel to your home, give him food and a bed – even help him find the next trade. Four months into the experiment, Shantanu found himself in New York City. It was there he realised that this experiment of his could really work.

He has travelled to every continent, welcomed by strangers into their homes, lives and communities.

What is Pixel Trade?

The Pixel Trade project was an experiment and exploration to see if it was possible to reach all seven continents without spending a cent of my own money on anything in the process.

What inspired you to travel the world without spending any money, and how long did you manage to travel without having any cash?

The inspiration came from a number of circumstances in my life, but it essentially boiled down to a desire to challenge everyday ideas, such as the barriers we put in place that create a perception that something is unachievable. Money was a big one. I love it – most people do – but I don't agree that it is as important as many of us think. The core of what money offers is amazing, but the dependencies and stress it can often build up are not. Perception was the main thing in question here.

After 1238 days, I managed to reach all seven continents without spending a cent.

What did you have in your backpack?

I think travelling with no money or very little money is associated with backpacking and hostels or couch surfing, but Pixel Trade wasn't that. I travelled well, I stayed in comfort and I ate like a king the majority of the time. I felt so privileged to see the world for such a long time without having to feel I was on a budget and watching my savings. The result was that I travelled with a big roller suitcase, camera bag and laptop bag. I didn't travel light. I didn't need to, most of the time. I had to be ready for every climate, so my bags were focused on equipment and versatility.

At what point during Pixel Trade did you realise, 'Hang on, this is going really well, I'm just going to keep doing this'?

It was always on and off. The first time I felt it was in New York City, around month four of the project. That place makes you feel like a rock star when it flows with you and a total washout when it doesn't. NYC was in my flow, and it gave me a boost of how unreal the life I was living truly was.

When you first started the project, how did you get offers for trades? And did the number of trades increase as your project went on?

All I needed to do was start with one trade. Part of the 'rules' was that the person I was trading with had to find me the next trade if I didn't have one, until which time I would be in their care. Word spread over time, and things started to get more demanding, which meant more emails and more organising. It was great because yes, I could be picky, but it also became more draining. By the final year of the project I was booked out four to six months ahead.

How did moving around so much change your relationship to place and nature?

Drastically. Political borders started to blur into one another. New places I had never seen started to feel familiar in a bizarre way, which for me wasn't a good thing because I would stop looking when it came to photographing my surroundings. I had to concentrate and remind myself how unique these places were.

> "
> It essentially boiled
> down to a desire to
> challenge everyday
> ideas, such as the
> barriers we put in
> place that create
> a perception
> that something is
> unachievable.

Nature became such an important refuge for me too. If I was disconnected for too long, my energy began to falter. By default it was easier for people in cities to trade with me, and therefore most of my trades happened around large metropolitan areas. A city is wild in a way that can suck your energy away. I didn't have a lot left to give, so I started holding nature as a liferaft.

Did living in foreign countries without money change the way you connected with each place?

I never looked into tourist attractions, shopping areas, bars, restaurants … anything that involved money, I wasn't interested in knowing about. I was brought to those environments with my trades, but I was more interested in exploring what the physical area offered, not the products and services therein. I was also lucky as my trades wanted to be great hosts and they knew the area they lived in better than someone who just passes through. They wanted to show me a good time, so I really got to experience things from a local perspective. Which to me is travel. My experience of a local's experience.

Did the people you trade with have a similar ethos on living and money?

Sometimes, but it was more about people who welcomed different forms of thinking. I traded with wealthy people and poor people. They are the same, in most ways. We forget that sometimes.

What is your current project?

The Honorarium Volumes. It is an idea that came from my last trade to Antarctica. The volumes are an ongoing collection of limited edition photographic artworks that focus on small interactions all over the world. Each volume is focused on a particular country and is funded by an audience who pre-purchases a print package or book.

..........x

> **"**
> A city is wild in a way that can suck your energy away. I didn't have a lot left to give, so I started holding nature as a liferaft.

Shantanu Starick travelled all over the world, experiencing landscapes like this one in Austria, but didn't spend a cent: instead he took photographs of people's homes and projects in exchange for room and board. In this way he saw all seven continents, discovering that money isn't the barrier we like to think it is.

A house in balance with nature

Michael Leung was an architect living a fast-paced life in London, working on big projects for even bigger clients. He moved to Byron Bay, on Australia's east coast, with his family in search of a slower kind of life. But what he found in the rolling hinterland of this patch of tropical New South Wales was more than just a relaxed pace; it was a personal housing revolution – in the form of hemp.

Michael used hemp to build his new home, Sky Farm, mixing it with sand and lime to form walls that sucked up carbon dioxide and released oxygen back into the air. Building with hemp allowed him to create a structure that was good for the environment and his family – a house that gave back as much as it took.

Building Sky Farm inspired him to try and spark a bigger change in the way we build. His company, Balanced Earth, believes in the power of natural and recycled materials and smart design to build dwellings that are actually good for the world.

After working as an architect in the United Kingdom for twenty-five years, I moved to Byron Bay with my family in search of more balance. My wife had come back from a trip to Peru and had a vision that we needed to move to Australia immediately, away from our fast-paced lives. That was where I built Sky Farm, a house made out of hemp, in the hills behind the town. We kept the name given to the land by the previous owners – from it, you can see the magical display of Mullumbimby's seasonal sky and farmland earth. Sky Farm keeps us connected with nature and feels like home for us. It's a wonderful feeling of security and wellbeing, knowing there are no toxic materials whatsoever in our family home.

Although there's a huge carbon punch involved in growing hemp, our hemp house is carbon negative. It keeps us warm in winter, while the cross-ventilation keeps us cool in summer. We rescued our windows from a house demolition, and the floorboards are factory seconds. We collect rainwater for drinking and have a composting toilet.

My family and I have a constant hinterland view from our house, which keeps us connected to the cycles of nature. We see every sunrise and sunset, and we experience the winds, rainy season and hot spells. It makes us feel safe and more in balance with the environment, as we have built with materials provided by Mother Nature and Earth itself.

I built Sky Farm in three months with Luke Wrencher and Ture Schmidt, who quickly became friends. I made a deep connection with them while building Sky Farm, and together we have founded Balanced Earth, a design and building company that cares about how we all live and breathe.

We truly believe that the health of our buildings affects the health of its inhabitants and our environments, and now we make homes that are in balance with our health and our planet. Our dream is to take hemp from paddock to place; we want to grow the hemp on the land the house will stand on, and to become seamless, sustainable and local.

..........x

> " Sky Farm keeps us connected with nature and feels like home for us. It's a wonderful feeling of security and wellbeing, knowing there are no toxic materials whatsoever in our family home.

Wild creations

Chef and adventurer Sarah Glover grew up in one of Australia's wildest places, surfing the turbulent waves of Tasmania, nibbling on berries from the bushes she passed. Fresh, local produce was always on her table and blooming in her backyard. With wilderness so close, she didn't have to go far for adventure.

The thrill of far-flung adventures was what drew her to the mainland, where she met people who inspired her love of surfing, travel and cooking for people. As she made her way up the coast of Australia, then on to New York City and back again, she helped open restaurants and design menus, learning about cooking along the way. She opened her own sweets shop in Bondi Beach, Australia, in 2009, spending her days in the surf and pouring herself into cooking and sharing.

The more people she met, the more she found that most of them hadn't grown up as wild as she had – had never known the joys that come from cooking outdoors with family and friends. So she wrote her *Wild Adventure Cookbook*, dedicated to the art and pleasures of cooking outdoors and over the campfire with good friends, local ingredients and the good that comes of letting nature inspire you.

You grew up in Tasmania – what was your childhood there like, and how did it influence your love of food and the outdoors?

Growing up on the island, I never thought twice about having fresh raspberries at my beck and call, or apricots that oozed with every golden, sun-filled bite. My backyard was full of fresh produce, which I could eat whenever my tummy grumbled, and the wild outdoors were at my doorstep. It wasn't so much of an influence as a way of living. You went outside on the weekends; you surfed rugged beaches and lit fires to keep warm.

It wasn't until I moved to the mainland that I started to realise that my experience having access to local, fresh produce was a rarity for most.

How does surfing inspire you?

Surfing is my time to clear my mind. It allows me to stop thinking about what I need to do or be and to just laugh and have fun. Fun and laughter are medicine – they motivate me. The friends I have met through the ocean have become lifelong mates who inspire me to be authentic.

What drew you to pack your bags and go up the coast of Australia, then over to America? What continues to drive you to go on adventures?

I am a thrill seeker – I can't help myself. I'm always trying to find a new challenge and hurdle to jump over, because it's an adrenaline rush. I just like creating and being on the road – it stimulates my creativity. I go home to sleep and rest, then I go out again.

You've worn many professional hats over the years, both food related and not. What keeps drawing you back to food?

I like to talk, to hear people's stories and share my passion with them. For me, cooking is about that exchange. Food is what I can offer people. I think it's that I get to be creative with my hands.

Food is something that nourishes and brings people together. It is a necessity of life, and I want to deliver it in a way that inspires people to gather. The campfire is a nonjudgmental environment – people take off their shoes and just relax. You don't find people looking at their phones around a fire!

> My backyard was full of fresh produce, which I could eat whenever my tummy grumbled, and the wild outdoors were at my doorstep. It wasn't so much of an influence as a way of living.

You talk about 'raw cooking' – being inspired not by a recipe, but by the ingredients you have to work with. What do you love about that approach to cooking?

I like the challenge of cooking with what I find on the road or at the markets, talking to the providers about their produce and what makes them happy. It's about the story and the connections you make. I come from a long line of farmers and fishermen, and the tales and stories they tell make the food taste better. Sounds weird, but it's true.

You have a cookbook that's all about wild cooking – the idea of cooking outside and out on adventures. What inspired that project? What do you hope your readers will take away from it?

I grew up living in the bush, playing up trees and eating food from the garden, so I think it was meant to be that my first book would pay homage to that way of life. It was so much fun just taking it outdoors, not knowing what I was going to cook, but just creating from the moment. I think that life has become too sterile. We have forgotten what it's like to get your hands dirty and let go of the rules.

What does nature mean to you and your work?

Without it, we wouldn't be able to breathe; we need the land to survive and we need to respect it! I wouldn't be doing what I am without it, so it's everything.
..........x

> "
> I think that life has become too sterile. We have forgotten what it's like to get your hands dirty and let go of the rules.

Mussels with salt water and potatoes

It's magical, making this dish by the sea with freshly caught mussels plucked straight from the rocks. We were on a beach on the east coast of Tasmania when we tried this method, at a little bay we'd discovered by accident. It was sheltered from the sea breeze, the perfect spot to light a campfire. I stoked the fire to a medium heat while preparing my mussels – once ready, I buried the pot in the coals. The air filled with a smoky aroma that drew my friends in from the beach to sit around and share a meal with the sea on our side.

Remember to pick mussels whose shells are securely closed and that are damp and shiny. If you have to purchase the mussels, don't pick any with broken, cracked or split shells. This dish is so easy; I promise you anyone can make it.

Serves 3

1 onion, finely diced

2 tomatoes, diced

3 salad rose potatoes (or another variety of red-skinned potato), skin on, cut into 1 cm (⅓ in) cubes

2 cups white wine

1 cup seawater

1 kg (2 lb 3 oz) mussels, cleaned and debearded

2 cloves fresh young garlic, diced (for garnish)

small handful of flat-leaf parsley, leaves picked and washed (for garnish)

Light a campfire and let it burn down until it's at medium heat.

Combine the onion and tomatoes in your billy or large pot and place them in the coals of the fire. Cook for about 1 minute, then add the potatoes, white wine and 1 cup seawater.

Cook for 20 minutes or until the potatoes are soft.

Add the mussels, then cover and cook until the mussels open up, discarding any that don't open (they are not good to eat).

Serve sprinkled with garlic and parsley. Eat at the beach and enjoy the salty air and salty mussels.

Campfire marshmallows

There's something comforting, something heartening, about putting a marshmallow on a stick and roasting it over a crackling fire until it's just bubbling on the outside, its skin turned toasty and fire-edged. You can make your own marshmallows before you leave home, which will give you the satisfaction of making it, as well as roasting it, yourself.

1 cup water

3 packets gelatine

2 cups white sugar

½ cup corn syrup

1 tbsp vanilla extract

1 tbsp peppermint extract

chocolate for a dark, gooey centre (optional)

icing sugar, for dusting

Get a slice tin ready by greasing it with butter and lining it with cling wrap.

Pour ½ cup of the water into a medium bowl. Add the gelatine, stir and set aside.

In a medium saucepan on high heat, place the sugar, corn syrup and the remaining ½ cup of water. Bring to the boil (you want it to roll with bubbles). Allow to boil for an additional minute, then remove from the heat. Add in the vanilla and peppermint extracts.

Using a handheld electric mixer, begin mixing the gelatine mixture. Slowly add the sugar syrup while you continue to mix on a low speed.

Once all sugar syrup is added, turn the mixer to high speed and whip for 10-12 minutes until the batter almost triples in size and becomes very thick. Scrape down the sides to prevent overflowing.

Transfer the mixture into your prepared slice tin – work fast, or it will set before it's all in the pan. If you like, you can pour only half of the mixture into the pan, then spread melted chocolate over it, leaving the edges white, and cover with the remaining mixture to create what will be gooey chocolate insides. Once you've finished pouring everything in, cover with more cling wrap and set the pan aside to set.

Once it is set, place icing sugar on a board, turn out the marshmallow and cut into chunks.

The shifting of tides

Tucked into Washington State's northwest corner, the Wilderness Coast is not named lightly. It is a wild place, a remote place, a rare coastline free from houses, cars, shops; a place that feels timeless even as the tides constantly remake it. Kate Armstrong and Paul Gablonski headed for this section of the world, wanting somewhere they could connect with each other and get away from the summer crowds. They planned to hike in and spend a night out on the beach. But they didn't expect that their plans would also be remade by the tides; that they would find a walk that tested them, awed them and showed them the rewards of getting off the well-formed path.

The trail Paul and I followed wasn't a trail at all. It was just slick rocks and windswept sand strung out over miles of rugged coastline, unmarked except for the occasional wooden sign. Unlike Olympic National Park's other trails, there was no way a ranger could tend or mend it. It shifted hour by hour, constantly being remade by the sea.

The ranger who'd sold us our hiking permits warned us that there were only small windows of time when the ocean dipped low enough to do the hike safely. Time it wrong, and we could get stranded or hurt. But it was just a beach, we reasoned: flat sand and a clear path to walk.

This coast is the United States' longest stretch of undeveloped coastline, bar Alaska: 117 kilometres (73 miles) that, for the most part, can only be accessed by foot. We planned to hike some 48 kilometres (30 miles) of it, from Shi Shi Beach to Cape Alava, where we'd spend the night before hiking back. We'd only done an overnight hike once before, but that didn't matter. I wanted a beautiful walk – a remote walk. A place that felt far away from the click of cameras and the jingling of bear bells that we could call our own for a night.

The first stretch of beach was flat and lovely, full of happy swimmers and people walking their dogs. Rocky sea stacks jutted out of the water just offshore. They looked like wild-wigged giants, topped with fuzzy patches of grass and pine. We gave them names to distract ourselves from the weight on our backs. I'd forgotten how a heavy pack throws you off balance, making you relearn how to move.

The beach got wilder after that first sandy stretch, dotted with shallow pools, shifting pebbles and slick tangles of seaweed. Eventually we ran out of beach and into the wall of a headland. There was a salt-hardened rope dangling down from a tree somewhere above us, and a sign nailed to its trunk marking it as an overland pass. I planted my feet against the crumbling cliff and climbed, hand over hand, fighting against the weight of my pack and the wind that tried to grab it. I was afraid of heights, but there was no way around it. The trail was *up*, so up we went.

From the top, we could see the full sweep of the ocean below us: white-fringed waves crashing like a living thing against the cliffs. We walked through dense, prehistoric-looking woodlands. We couldn't always see the ocean then, but we could hear it, swishing and sighing like a hot-air balloon being filled. All coastlines were like this once; wild and winding, untamed by boat or hand.

We descended back to the beach by rope, walked across it, climbed another headland. Again and again, until we reached a tiny beach and another headland. It offered no rope; no sign; no more trail to walk along. We decided to rest there, thinking that the tide just needed time to go out. I dropped my pack and stared at the ocean, musing about how it goes in and out, like living breath. Ceaseless.

Three hours later, we figured out what was wrong. The tide wasn't going out – it was coming in, threatening to trap us. We hurriedly put our packs back on and moved towards the base of the headland. The only way to move forward was to find a way to go around it, over the piles of rock and boulder between it and the surging waves.

We climbed from rock to rock for what felt like hours, cutting our hands on shells and seaweed until we reached the next beach. But there was no flat sand – just an avalanche of ever-sliding pebbles half as big as our heads. Then more unclimbable headland, more boulders, more tide.

The ocean was rising, rising with each wave as the tide came in; how high up would it come? Would it swallow us? One slip with this much weight on my back and I could easily break a bone. Strand myself in the middle of a place where it could take days for someone to find us. It was nerve-fraying, foot-cracking, skin-splitting work. I didn't want to keep moving. But, like the ocean, it was all I could do.

By the time we reached a flat stretch of beach, sandy and blessedly even, it was well past eight in the evening. We saw no one else, and no campsite. So we threw off our packs at an abandoned fire pit and pitched our tiny tent. It was just us and the seals on that rock-strewn beach.

> **"**
> I was afraid of heights, but there was no way around it. The trail was *up*, so up we went.

"
I dropped my pack and
stared at the ocean,
thinking about how it
goes in and out, like living
breath. Ceaseless.

> **Every minute painted the sky in fresh colours, stretching in wings of pink and purple and red. It stained everything: the sand, the sea stacks, our skin, the seals barking at each other in the shallows.**

Sitting there, exhausted and speechless, we watched the most beautiful sunset I've ever seen. Every minute painted the sky in fresh colours, stretching in wings of pink and purple and red. It stained everything: the sand, the sea stacks, our skin, the seals barking at each other in the shallows. All the more beautiful because it was earned. It made it so the frayed nerves of the day no longer mattered. We fell asleep unbothered by the rocky ground.

We left before seven the next morning, having learnt our lesson about obeying our tide chart, and found a different trail than we remembered. The low tide created new, more solid paths to follow. Our footsteps were the only ones in the sand. It felt like we were the only two people who had ever been here – a world so quiet that we could hear the soft sigh of sand being pulled by the tide, the *whomp* of an eagle's wings, the crackling of tiny insects leaping through the fat piles of kelp.

That's part of the beauty of overnight hikes. Your world becomes small enough that there is nothing at all between you and what's around you. You know what you're eating for dinner, because it's in your pack. You know where you're going, because it's marked on your map. There's nothing but the burn of your muscles, the weight on your back, and the beauty of the world. Except your mind, unshackled from your everyday worries and free to wander over thoughts about the movement of oceans, the age of rocks and the slant of the sun.

When we got back to our car, we were tired and filthy. It was the hardest hike I had ever done, the most lost I had ever felt. But I couldn't stop smiling. That is the magic of walking out into wilderness, carrying your whole world on your back.

..........x

The joys of growing, trading, sustaining

It was the prospect of living a real life – a full life – that enticed Lentil and Matt Purbrick to quit their jobs in the city and move to the Australian country. They were after something different, a chance to connect with food, people, time and nature. They fixed up a derelict old house that overlooked a billabong and planted a world that grew and grew and grew. They shared this world through their food, their trades, and their blogging – inspiring thousands of others to think about how they, too, could live a more sustainable life.

You live in a house on a pocket of a bigger property. What's the house like, and what sort of state was it in when you found it?

Matt and I live in a very old farmhouse; it was originally built in 1940. It's a cute little weatherboard cottage that overlooks the property's backwater, which is like a billabong (a small, quiet water hole). The house is full of white walls, wood, a little bit of art from people we love, a whole lot of pottery, books and linen. It's just got the simple things that we love. It's surrounded by a hectare (2.5 acres) of cleared land, where we grow all of our produce and keep our animals, and just over a hectare of native bush.

I still remember what the house and property was like before we moved in. We actually had to climb in through the window because there wasn't a key for the door. It was so run-down that the power points were coming out of the walls, many of which were cracked, and it was filled with old linoleum floors and a bathroom that looked like it had walked straight out of a '60s motel (and not in a good way). The outside had so many sheds that people had half-built over the years and heaps of junk. But it had a great feeling about it, so we cleaned it up and made it ours.

Did you fix it up yourself?

We renovated it ourselves, quickly, over one winter. We wanted to get the farm planted before the summer, so we made it happen. We basically just ripped out a whole heap of stuff to bring it back to a simple shell, took out a few walls to open it up, painted it white and filled it with wooden benches and a deck. We took out all of the sheds that blocked our view of the billabong and repurposed (or got rid of) the materials that were lying around. Then we built our garden and moved our animals in! We made it an open, functional space, and we really opened it up to the outside so it was much more connected to the land it was on.

Did you move to the house with the aim of becoming self-sustaining, or did you sort of make it up as you went along?

I wouldn't say we are truly self-sustaining: it's not really something we see as achievable or realistic. We definitely believe in doing what you can, and sharing/trading your abundance with the 'village' so everyone has what they need.

> **"**
> The main aim, always, is that we work with nature – what it is doing at any given time.

"

We see our lives ruled by nature, our lives change with nature – rather than the other way around.

But yes, we definitely made it up as we went along, to a point. I think you have to – you only know what you know at any given time. As you learn, you become more open to different ideas, your perspective changes and your passion for different things develops. We learnt and experimented with all of the things we could do ourselves. The main thing for us was, and still is, the *experience* of it – growing, gathering, nurturing animals, trading, making what we could. That's what it is all about. This, for us, is just so rewarding and life-changing.

How do you run your property?

The main aim, always, is that we work with nature – what it is doing at any given time. We see it as a dance: it does this, you do that. You are always watching it and responding to it. We think that agriculture, as a rule, has become too controlling. It is not so much about cooperating with nature anymore as it is about dominating and enslaving it. So we try to keep things a bit wilder. We try to give our animals what they need and then let them live according to their instincts, not our constant interference. It's the same with our plants. We try to just give them the optimal conditions to thrive naturally, and then we let them grow and do their thing, again interfering as little as possible.

It means less work for us and provides us with incredible results. We're not doing anything more or less special than constantly observing our plants and animals and ensuring they have everything they need. There aren't any rules, just simple observation and response.

Has working the land changed your connection with nature?

It has one hundred per cent changed it. We see our lives ruled by nature, our lives change with nature – rather than the other way around.

This is how we have come to understand the world. Whether we are at home or travelling, we are always observing – looking for what's flowering around us, what fruit is ripening, what insects are doing. We understand the time of year, the season, the climate. It's how we make sense of things all the time and live *with* nature.

What is an average day on the farm?

Unlike what many may think, we take the mornings slow. We have a juice, a coffee or a tea and make a slow breakfast. Then we get out there and do what needs to be done – it can be anything from planting seeds, harvesting, gathering from the wild, tending to the animals. It is always changing,

> " Everything feels abundant – it just feels as though we have so *much*. So much to be grateful for, so much beauty, so much food around us. It's hard to get that until you surround yourself with nature.

depending on the time of year. We just know, based on what time of year it is, what needs to be done.

We try to limit our time on computers and only check our emails twice a week. But we also love projects – we are, at heart, artists. So we write, draw, paint, do pottery, dance, photograph. Some of this we get paid for or trade for, and some we just do for fun. This also inspires our outside time – it all fits together.

Besides growing your own food, you also cook it and sometimes even trade it – how important is it to you to create and share things made with your own hands?

Very. This is where the joy is at; to us, it is what makes life fun. If we can't grow or produce something ourselves, then having a direct relationship with the people who do is important to us because we've seen how enriching that experience is.

If someone took away our ability to cook, trade, feast, I truly think we would become very depressed. Those shared experiences are what life's all about!

How do you feel stepping out of the door in the morning and seeing the land that you work on?

Peaceful, and as if we can breathe. Everything feels abundant – it just feels as though we have so *much*. So much to be grateful for, so much beauty, so much food around us. It's hard to get that until you surround yourself with nature. Nature is naturally abundant, whereas the urban environment can feel inherently competitive.

Your journey has become famous through your blog, social media, events and now your book, and you've become advocates for a more sustainable way of living. How does that advocacy shape what you do?

It's probably the other way around; all of our decisions have shaped our advocacy. Whom we work with, what we choose to do in our everyday lives, how we travel and the stories we share have always had sustainable values at their core. It's something we've always embraced in all aspects of our lives. It's like art to us. It's our passion and something we live for.

We truly believe in what we do and we genuinely live by what we advocate. But we are not driven by our advocacy.

We are driven simply by the aim to live a good life. It just so happens that in living a good life we seem to be inspiring others to make positive changes in theirs. We feel super lucky by how all that has turned out.

At the end of the day, what makes you satisfied?

Feeling satisfied in all of life's small moments. Feeling grateful for everything we have and all of the experiences that make up life – a morning coffee, harvesting some tomatoes, smelling fresh air, love, people, plants, cooking …

This is our measure: if we are doing things that make us feel negative or we aren't enjoying, we stop. It's about the everyday things for us.

..........x

Lentil and Matt Purbrick moved from the city to the country, transforming an old, run-down property Into the farmhouse of their dreams. It's there they learnt how to live with nature, devoting their days to growing their own food, tending their animals, and boiling life down to its simplest pleasures.

Following the forager's path

Walking into the woods on a foraging expedition isn't about conquering the wilderness or taking from it: to Heather Hillier, it's about living in harmony with its ebbs and flows, its seasons and its life cycle, feeling your way along paths that others have trodden before. It's part of living an intentional life, one that Heather cultivated on a self-sustaining farm she ran before leaving it behind to travel to Argentina on a motorbike (see page 109). She forages to live, to learn from nature, and to experience the aches and pains that come from finding your own food.

When the first of our species took their initial steps out of forest and into grassland, they made a path of footprints for us. They began a network of trails and left an inescapable legacy: the hunger for discovery. This urge has come to define our relationships, to each other as well as the wilderness.

That path has now been paved, and you're either flying down it in a car or you're being left behind. Wilderness is separate, untouched, only for viewing from the road at a safe distance and venturing into with the right gear; all for an experience, something to be gained or won, and surely deserved.

Yet there are narrow paths that still remain, etched into dark forests and sprawled over prairies, leading us back into our own natures. They twist and wind and weave us; the need to walk down them rushes through every artery. The wilderness does not ask if we are male or female, urban or rural. It knows of our competence and, in return, asks us to know it and love it.

I want to know this world, to insert myself into its story. I want to know the organisms that I interact with, consciously or not. I want to forage from the earth and embrace my wildness. We are, all of us, taking and giving, foraging and creating, weaving a web of interdependency with nature that I take care to acknowledge as I walk into the forest.

I want to feel the sting of a nettle; see blood dried on scratched-up legs from searching for sun-warmed blackberries; feel the ache as I stoop, scanning the forest floor for mushrooms, hair caught in an endless tangle of branches. I want to feel the pull of an outgoing current as I dive deeply into a cold, dark sea, and the rush of adrenaline as frozen hands and feet thaw – a painful reminder that I am alive. For it means I will eat. I will live.

This wilderness is not pristine – it has been touched too many times. It is, however, perfect; perfectly changing, resetting, giving and taking. Foraging gives us understanding of nature and our dependence on it; it makes the food we eat real, the source transparent. This knowledge of nature and its cycles will guide our feet into the breathtaking beauty of the wild. Our hearts, unquestionably, will follow.

..........x

> ❝
> We are, all of us, taking and giving, foraging and creating, weaving a web of interdependency with nature that I take care to acknowledge as I walk into the forest.

> This wilderness is not pristine ... it is, however, perfect.

An escape to the soul of the surf

Soul & Surf, a yoga and surf retreat, started as the dream of two time-harassed Londoners. Ed and Sofie Templeton felt the call of a life lived away from deadlines, focused on the things that made them feel content: yoga, surfing, good friends and good food. So they quit their jobs, left the city and travelled around the world for a year. They eventually found themselves in Kerala, India, surfing uncrowded waves where no one was lined up behind them waiting to catch the next break. They invited a few people to come and stay, and before long it turned into Soul & Surf. The retreat isn't just meant as a travel experience in a beautiful place – for Ed and Sofie, it is a new way of living.

Was there any particular moment where you just went, 'that's it, I've got to quit my job and travel'?

I'd been running a graphic design company for fourteen years, designing album covers for the likes of Fatboy Slim and Elbow, and films for Playstation, to name a few projects. I had also been a DJ for sixteen years, but that career kind of fizzled out when I became too tired to stay up all night DJing and then design all day. Sofie had been working hard in the fashion industry, and we met one another at a time when we'd both become disillusioned with the relentless, deadline-chasing creative worlds, and were both ready for a new adventure.

On a trip to Panama early in our relationship, we did a kind of 'blue sky' exercise, writing down how we'd like to spend our days if we won millions of dollars and didn't have to worry about work or money. Having defined that, we worked back from there to see how we could live that lifestyle *without* the millions. Soul & Surf was one amongst many of the possibilities we came up with.

Buoyed by these ideas, we came back to the United Kingdom, quit our jobs, sold the design company, rented the house out and set off on a year-long, ten-pounds-a-day surf and yoga adventure. We began with a road trip through France, Spain and Portugal before dropping the campervan off at home and flying to India, where we scoured the west coast for waves. We stayed in Varkala for a couple of months, surfing empty waves every day. We then went to Bali and Lombok (Indonesia), then Australia and on to Central America.

Soul & Surf began as an extension of this round-the-world trip, to buy us six more months somewhere warm over winter. We started small, inviting people to come and stay at our house in Kerala and do the things we love to do: surf, eat great food, hang out and practise yoga … oh, and have a little party here and there. We like to live a balanced life with equal measures of health and fun.

> "
> We started small, inviting people to come and stay at our house in Kerala and do the things we love to do: surf, eat great food, hang out and practise yoga … oh, and have a little party here and there.

What attracted you to Kerala initially, and then to Ahangama, Sri Lanka?

On our round-the-world trip we scoured the west coast of India for waves and somewhere to settle for a month or two – we felt at home when we arrived in Varkala, in the state of Kerala. It had empty waves, an amazing, vibrant temple nearby, and a good balance of amenities and restaurants for a Western palate without losing a sense of living in a Kerala community. And we made some good local friends pretty quickly too. Once we had set up and were working regularly in Kerala, we took our short breaks away in Sri Lanka, a forty-minute hop by plane. We really got to know and appreciate the south coast. Sri Lanka is a very different place to India: more developed for tourists, with lots more surfers. But when you scratch beneath the surface and head inland a couple of kilometres from the busy coastal strip, you find the real Sri Lanka: quiet, beautiful, wild and rich in culture and wildlife. There is definitely a deep soul in both of these places.

When you landed in Kerala, what made you decide to start a retreat that's about yoga and surfing, as opposed to one or the other?

It was pure selfishness. And pure luck. It's become the latest trend to do surfing and yoga together, but the honest answer is that I am a surfer who enjoys yoga, Sofie's a yogi who enjoys surfing and we both enjoy travel and to entertain friends. In setting up India's first surf and yoga retreat, we got to do the things we love on a daily basis with a load of cool people from around the world.

Do you still feel the need to get out there on a daily surf, do something for yourself as opposed to the business? Do you have a special spot where you like to go?

During our really crazy, chaotic start-up or crisis management periods (these are regular occurrences when operating in challenging environments), I have to remember what we are here for and why we are doing Soul & Surf. If we don't live and breathe what we offer our guests, then what is the point? An hour or two in the surf, an hour or so on the mat, or an hour on the massage table are all special, wherever we happen to be.

Soul & Surf seems to be very much about connecting with the local environment and community in both India and Sri Lanka. Is that a big part of your business?

Before we set up, while we were travelling, we heard some bad stories about Western exploitation in some of the bigger, better-known surf destinations. We promised ourselves that if we ever set up a business in a place like that we would do all we could to break that cliché. One of our core company values is and has always been that if and when we leave an area, we leave a positive legacy behind. In Kerala, that has manifested in a few ways: we have taught as many local people and kids to surf as we can and developed that into a weekly surf club. We now employ some of these kids in our cafe, and some have joined our team of instructors. This season, we have finally achieved what we always wanted: a fully qualified, fully professional, well-paid, Kerala-born team of surf instructors.

What do you hope people achieve by the end of their stay with Soul & Surf?

A nice time. Or the inspiration to change the way they live their lives. But anywhere in between is good for us.

..........x

> In setting up India's first surf and yoga retreat, we got to do the things we love on a daily basis.

Under star-flecked skies

For Stephanie Francis, Homecamp's sister company Under Sky is all about re-introducing people to the good life: sleeping outdoors, gathering around a fire and connecting with nature while surrounded by great friends and bright stars. The whole idea behind this outdoor events company is that camping shouldn't be suffered through or an exercise in deprivation and a bad night's sleep. By taking the work out of camping, making it feel a little bit luxurious, she aims to help people remember how to let go of the city rush and embrace the simple joy of being out in nature – the memories that can only be made around a roaring fire. They set up their camps in unique locations: private properties and beautiful fields that most people would not otherwise have access to, reminding them that natural beauty isn't only remote and wild.

When she held their first Under Sky event in a private olive grove, surrounded by the low-slung mountains of a national park, she saw first-hand the magic that happens when busy people step away from the daily grind, towards a beautiful canvas tent and an open sky.

From the trees in the olive grove, I watched over the peaks of the northern Grampians National Park in central Victoria, Australia, the rocks changing colours as the sun began to set. A few stars started to appear, promising a special stargazing night ahead.

Our guests were beginning to gather around the communal campfire, sharing glasses of wine, rugging up, enjoying the view. Barbecues were being lit and conversations were starting. Our canvas bell tents were set perfectly, offering everyone a comfortable, cosy room for the night.

With the stars above us and the warm glow of camaraderie wrapped around us, I knew we'd created something special.

Under Sky is all about creating these moments and helping them grow. We had always prided ourselves on our camp setups at festivals, which is where the idea was born. We wanted to create unforgettable outdoor experiences, offering people luxe tent accommodation to encourage them to get out of their homes and out into nature. To show them that being in nature can be comfortable as well as exhilarating; indulgent as well as simple.

This camping adventure in the Grampians was the first time we tried out our nomadic hotel concept, where we choose magical properties and open them up to the public.

The stunning Mount Zero Olive Grove at the base of the Grampians offered guests the unique experience of camping in an olive grove, surrounded by spectacular views of rocky peaks and with easy access to one of Australia's most beautiful parks. The olive grove is a private property, which so few city dwellers ever get to experience. Though it's a working place, a tended place, it has a wildness all its own.

We try to make our guests as comfortable as possible, but we also encourage a connection to the natural world and a separation from their hectic lives in the city. The whole point is to enable urban people to experience the joy of camping without all of the hard work associated with it.

Campfire conversations and woodfired pizza; stargazing from under the olive trees; crawling into a cosy tent (proper bed and all!) to fall asleep under canvas. This is what memories are made of. This is why Under Sky exists.

..........X

"
The olive grove is a private property, which so few city dwellers ever get to experience. Though it's a working place, a tended place, it has a wildness all its own.

“
We wanted to stay there for a long time, to get the feeling of living there, not just visiting.

The heart of darkness

....

Inge Wegge was born into the cold, wild places of the world and feels called to document their precarious beauty.

His first film, *North of the Sun*, was made with his friend Jørn Ranum in 2012 and followed their stay on a remote, uninhabited cove off the north coast of Norway, far north of the Arctic Circle where the sun disappears for months at a time. Even though this beach was in the far reaches of the world, it was covered in pieces of plastic that had washed ashore. They built a hut from this material and settled down to live through the dark winter, surfing and attempting to clean up the beach.

But Inge was not finished with these wild yet tarnished places. In his second film, *Bear Island*, Inge travelled to the uninhabited Bear Island to surf with his brothers Hakon and Markus. While the brothers were told to leave no trace, they arrived to beaches already covered in trash. In Inge's film, we voyeur on the fate of these places where humans leave a trace without making a footprint.

Tell us about yourself and where you live.

I live on the island of Lofoten in Norway. It's a paradise for me. It has everything I can dream of: mountains for skiing, snowboarding and climbing, good waves for surfing, and the people here are really nice. We live on an island, and island people tend to take care of each other.

My fantastic and inspiring wife is also into surfing and climbing, so we often do things together out in nature. Our daughter is three years old, and we have a second child coming soon. I'm really looking forward to taking them on adventures.

How did you come up with the idea for your first film, *North of the Sun*?

My friend from film school and I had both been to this amazing beach and seen all the trash and materials laying around. It inspired us to live there, building a house from the things that had washed ashore. We wanted to stay there for a long time, to get the feeling of *living* there, not just visiting. We knew the waves were surfable and we wanted to stay over one winter season so we could really enjoy it.

Both of your films feature places that few humans have ever set foot on, and yet they're covered in human-made waste. How do you feel when you arrive at a remote, wild place to find it covered in trash?

It's sad. It makes me realise how much plastic there must be in our oceans. Only a small part of it ends up on the beaches; the rest is just floating around, being crushed into smaller and smaller pieces, ending up inside fish and animals that might become our food someday.

***North of the Sun* is an adventure story, but there is also a strong environmental message. Was that unintentional, or was that part of the plan?**

It came naturally. The place is so beautiful, but I felt sad seeing all the plastic washed up on the beach. We wanted to clean everything. Absolutely everything. So we started picking up the pieces. But when we dug down into the sand, we discovered that it was just layers and layers of plastic. And new trash just kept coming in, every day. We realised that we could never take it all away. We wanted to make people aware of it and inspire them to try and make a difference.

In what way does 'giving back to nature' enhance an adventure, particularly in such a remote part of the world?

Nature gives me so many good moments. We wanted to give something back to it – not just consume what it offered. There was something about the feeling of a clean beach at the end of all that work. It made me feel that I had earned the right to call the bay my home.

Most surfers seek out tropical islands for their surf trips, but for *Bear Island* you chose what must be one of the world's coldest. Why did you choose it?

Warm places are tempting, but we don't know that much about snakes and mosquitoes and stuff. We are used to the cold, so it was natural for us to look north. Maybe it's a Norwegian thing, exploring cold places. Bear Island looked like the perfect place. It's a small island, only 15 kilometres (9 miles) wide and 20 kilometres (12 miles) long, so we had the chance to explore the whole coastline. Its mountains looked perfect for playing in the snow.

There's a moment in *Bear Island* when you talk about waves only existing for one moment in time, so to surf them is to coexist with that one pulse of the ocean's power. What does nature's power teach you?

When I'm out for a long time, I realise things that might feel important in everyday life – answering emails, staying updated on social media – really aren't. I also see more details in nature and become more open to its impressions. Living a rich life with simple means. Surfing is special because there is so much power in a wave, and becoming one with that energy makes me so focused. It makes every second feel like ten.

..........X

"

There was something about the feeling of a clean beach at the end of all that work. It made me feel that I had earned the right to call the bay my home.

Inge Wegge and Jørn Ranum chose to live on a sunless, frigid beach in northern Norway because they wanted to truly get to know it. They built their house out of the trash that had washed up on shore, then spent their days surfing and cleaning up a place that, for a while, came to feel like home.

Alone in the woods

Although Alison Kraner grew up in the woods of America's Mid-Atlantic region, coming to know its many sounds and hidden trails, she had never spent a night alone there. So when she signed up for a week-long leadership program, knowing that she would spend her final night by herself in the woods, she imagined how it would be – how it would feel. What she didn't imagine was that the woods would be so unfamiliar, filled with unexplained noises coming from things she couldn't see. The trick was to get comfortable with the woods again, to become a part of this newly made world.

We walked up from the clearing in the middle of the camp's farm. We didn't talk, but listened to our shoes hitting the trail as tall grasses and the beating Maryland sun gave way to dirt under our feet and the shade of the forest. After ten minutes or so down a narrow trail, I stopped in a small clearing while the others kept moving.

I dropped my backpack onto the ground and it echoed against the forest packed in around me. I was alone, equipped with a borrowed pack filled with peanut butter sandwiches and a bottle of water, a tarp I sort of knew how to set up, sleeping gear, a headlamp and an emergency whistle I was instructed not to use because it had never been cleaned.

Once their footsteps faded, I took a moment to stand as still as I could. I heard familiar voices: leaves whistled as they swept each other. Crickets and birds spoke. I could hear the river move somewhere below me, steady as it coaxed its way over rocks.

The forest here was dense, thick with large green leaves. I shivered despite the heat. For a while I tried to distract myself, playing with the tension in the ropes attached to my tarp, eating my sandwiches in small bites, taking careful sips of water.

The woods, stripped of the crack of my own shoes over branches and the clatter of those familiar voices, held the buzzing of a new world, one full of its own motions and patterns. But there were noises that I couldn't quite place. Branches popped under invisible weights that were gone as quickly as they had come; calls rang out around me, impossible to tell where one ended and another began.

After hours of twisting my head this way and that, seeking out the source of noises, I was exhausted. There was only one option: I had to let the unfamiliarity of this place settle over me, to become part of its rhythm. As the sun dipped its way into dark, the woods shed its humidity and learnt to breathe again, and I tried to breathe with it.

In one night, I did not learn to be comfortable alone in the woods, but I started to adjust to discomfort, to distinguish between fear and actual danger. Slowly, I let the surrounding noise settle within me until I found quiet. In the dark, I had built a world full of my own thoughts and fears. I let that go, learning to get comfortable with the real world of unknowns that surrounded me.

..........X

As the sun dipped its way into dark, the woods shed its humidity and learnt to breathe again, and I tried to breathe with it.

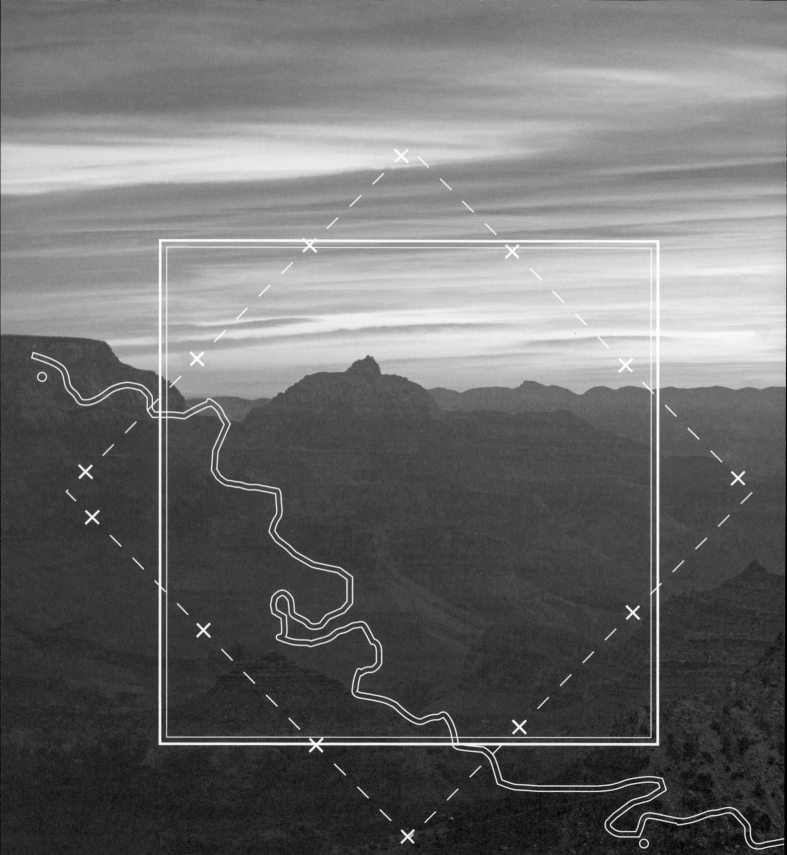

Nature's many compositions

Bec Kilpatrick grew up photographing the ocean and sugarcane fields of Byron Bay in New South Wales, Australia, on her dad's old Canon film camera. It was the start of her love of photography, which she developed at school, holing away in the darkroom at lunch and watching as the chemical process unveiled the scenes she had captured. She found that photography wasn't just about the magic of capturing a moment, but also about process, planning and practice. Once she started travelling, she discovered that taking her art on the road and out into nature helped her connect with her surroundings and inspire others to do the same.

Can you tell us about your work as a nature photographer?

All of my work begins with wanting to explore something in greater detail: a landscape through the lens of my camera, or the small textures of a bird's feather when I draw. A lot of my photography is based around nature, but also how we interact with it. I also shoot a lot of weddings, and try to draw and paint as much as I can. It's quite busy and transient, but I wouldn't want it any other way. My photographs often capture some sort of adventure, whether it's driving across the country, hiking in the mountains or exploring a new landscape in a new country. My biggest drive to photograph comes from seeing and experiencing a new place.

You're an illustrator as well. How do these two artistic practices differ and align?

Whether I'm taking photos or drawing, both processes involve me quietly observing and trying to represent a subject

> " I never regret travelling to a new place. You always learn so much from the environment you step into and the people you meet.

in a new way for people to enjoy. While both influence each other and demand the same patience, they do have their differences. With a photograph, you are bound by what you put in the frame; it is a constant challenge to create new perspectives and interesting compositions. When drawing, you are limitless. Whatever comes into your mind is possible, and that freedom can be liberating or terrifying. For me, it's important to have balance, to keep inspired and play with the way both mediums interact with each other.

Where do you live, and what do you enjoy about splitting your time between two continents?

I grew up in Byron Bay and will always call the sound of waves home. I travelled to Canada when I was twenty-one, where I fell in love with mountains (and Andrew, my partner). Since then we have moved between Calgary and Byron Bay, shooting weddings in the summers and working on travel and lifestyle jobs. More recently, we've been setting up market booths across Canada, selling our artwork and photographs. It has been such a fun and refreshing way to interact with people and share our art. These days it's so easy to get caught up with posting online and feeling disconnected with the work you are putting out. By getting out in the community and talking with other artists, we feel a greater connection with the work we are creating – it gives it meaning. We are so lucky to be able to split our time between two countries and work year-round doing what we love (with lots of time for exploring, too).

What's a normal day like for you?

Every day begins with a cup of tea! Sometimes it's in bed with my favourite cup, and other times it's in a travel mug on a long road trip. My favourites are made on a camp stove on top of a mountain after watching a beautiful sunrise.

I really struggle to impose structure on my day-to-day life, as freelancing can leave you always working. I'm always trying to figure out the best balance between creating new work, travelling for content, keeping up-to-date with websites and social content, and meeting my deadlines.

Your shots of nature are incredible and inspire us to dream of new places – how much work goes into each shot?

I never regret travelling to a new place. You always learn so much from the environment you step into and the people you meet. If I can convince someone looking at my photos to get outside and explore something outside their comfort zone, then that's amazing.

There's always a lot of planning that goes into photography, particularly in the realm of seeking out good locations. I am always researching to figure out when the light will be best, when the sun rises or sets, where the moon is and just generally keeping up-to-date on what the weather is doing. You have to set yourself up so that the unpredictable and unknown can create the magic shots.

How important is nature to your work?

As important as it is to my wellbeing. I never identified with life in the city; I either wanted to be an artist or a biologist when I grew up. The patterns, systems and cycles that exist in nature are fascinating, and I have fallen in love with documenting and interpreting them in my work. It's so nice to be reminded to stop and notice the little things that often go unnoticed in our world every day.

Where do you go in nature when you need to recharge?

When I'm at home in Australia, straight to my local beach. There's nothing more comforting than going for a swim in the ocean and losing my thoughts on the horizon. On the other hand, my ideal escape is to go on a long camping adventure in the mountains. I'm so grateful to have been able to spend so much time exploring the Rocky Mountains in Canada. There is nothing more grounding than packing a bag full of food and camping gear and sleeping under the stars for a few nights. It's the perfect way to reset your mind about the things that really matter, and it's where I feel most inspired.

> "
> There is nothing more grounding than packing a bag full of food and camping gear and sleeping under the stars for a few nights. It's the perfect way to reset your mind about the things that really matter, and it's where I feel most inspired.

What are some of your top tips for taking great photographs in nature?

First, the time of day is crucial. The best light comes in the early morning and late afternoon when the sun is low and soft. In order to take advantage of this light, you need to plan your days around it. Be prepared to be out late and get up early, and always pack a headlamp for those moments when you're setting up or heading back to camp after getting your shot!

Remember that the perfect shot requires planning, but make sure to plan for the unexpected. I put so much planning into capturing a 'perfect' shot, but some of my favourite images have come out of crazy adventures on little to no sleep! Like when planning out how to get a shot of the Emerald Lakes along the Tongariro Crossing on New Zealand's North Island (pictured at right). I read it was a three-hour hike from the carpark to the Red Crater, the highest point of the Crossing, and its spectacular view of the three turquoise-coloured volcanic lakes. We wanted to catch the first light hitting the lakes with no one around, so we began our hike around three in the morning to make sure we had plenty of time to hike up and find the perfect spot to set up our tripods. It was pitch black with no moon to guide us, my headlamp was running out of battery power and the wind was intense. We pushed through regardless and ended up getting to the top of the Red Crater around five: an hour-and-a-half before the sun was set to rise. We huddled together, trying to stay warm, when all of a sudden some hot air hit us. We thought we were losing our minds until we remembered that we were on volcanic land, which was steaming. When the sun finally rose over the volcanoes, we got the most beautiful photographs of the first light on the lakes and the steam rising in the foreground. It was a magical morning.

Make sure to get to know your camera and how to use it in different conditions. There's something to be said for the phrase, 'The best camera is the one you have with you'. Most people carry around pretty good cameras in their pockets every day – their phones! Smartphones do take great photos, but if you want to go beyond that and learn how to control and manipulate an image, a DSLR is a must.

DSLR means 'Digital Single Lens Reflex' or, to put it more simply, a camera that uses mirrors and interchangeable lenses. They aren't cheap or light, but the quality and control of the images gives it an advantage over any other compact camera. Using a DSLR allows you to control the shutter speed, aperture and overall exposure of your image. Controlling the shutter speed allows you to manipulate how long the digital sensor is exposed to light, allowing you to freeze or drag movement. Controlling the aperture allows you to adjust the diameter of the opening that lets light in. The lower the aperture, the wider the opening. For example, F1.8 lets more light in than F22, and it allows you to use the camera in low light situations. Once you learn how to use shutter speed and aperture, you can make sure your image is exposed properly for your environment.

There is no 'best' setting for your camera: just the most appropriate for a given situation. You always have to be ready to manually adjust your settings to the ever-changing environment. If the wind suddenly picks up on top of a mountain, it helps to switch your camera to Shutter Priority at a speed of at least 1/500 of a second. Shutter Priority, labelled 'TV' on your camera, allows you to choose a shutter speed and will automatically pick the correct aperture. This setting makes sure you have a shutter speed fast enough to overcome the camera shake caused by heavy winds. There's nothing worse than getting back to your computer and realising your photos aren't sharp!

Think about composition. It's easy to just point and shoot when you're in a beautiful place, but it's worth pausing to think about framing your shot. Take a second to note your surrounds: what objects or shapes make up the foreground? Would the photo be more interesting with someone in the frame to show scale? What lines are naturally present to lead your eye through the image?

In a traditional landscape photo, you have three fields of view: the foreground, the middle ground and the background. You can guide the viewer's eye to each of these areas using different techniques. The most popular is the rule of thirds, which I will talk about below. You can also use a low aperture to make sure only one field of view is in focus, isolating the focal point of the image: for instance, keeping

the middle ground with a lighthouse in focus but blurring the foreground (rocks) and background (sky). Another way you can direct the focus is by using the natural lines in the landscape to 'lead the eye through the image'.

There are a lot of compositional rules in photography that I think should be explored, then broken. The most popular is the rule of thirds, where you visually split up your image into a grid of nine squares and place your focal point at one of the horizontal and vertical intersections. The focal point is what you want the viewer to focus on first – it creates a powerful image. For landscape photography, it's nice to play with this rule by putting the horizon either in the top third or bottom third of your image. Try and avoid putting your horizon in the centre – use the grid to experiment with where you place it. For instance, if you want to capture a surfing photo, you could have the sea horizon running along the top third, the sun setting in the top left intersection and the surfer paddling on the bottom right intersection (this would be the main focal point).

When framing a shot, the main thing I think about is simplicity. It's often challenging to try and strip a busy landscape scene back to something uncluttered and captivating, but I think the most powerful images are often the simplest ones.

> **"**
> I put so much planning into capturing a 'perfect' shot, but some of my favourite images have come out of crazy adventures on little to no sleep!

Try out different lenses. There are two different types of lenses for DSLR cameras: fixed and zoom. Fixed, also called a prime lens, has just one focal length, which you cannot adjust. It tends to focus more quickly and produce sharper images, although you have less freedom when it comes to composition. A zoom lens is made with a focal range so you can shift in and out, which allows you more control when it comes to framing your image – much better for landscape photography.

There are lenses made for specific uses, like wide-angle for shooting landscapes and telephoto for shooting wildlife, but it's important to experiment. Don't always reach for your wide-angle lens; some of my favourite photos have come from trying out a telephoto lens.

Use a tripod. A tripod is essential for minimising camera shake and ensuring your images are nice and crisp, especially when taking photos in low light when the shutter needs to be open for longer in order to let in enough light to get a good image. You can also use your camera's settings to create some lovely stylistic effects when using your tripod. For example, if you are shooting water, stabilising your camera on a tripod lets you leave your shutter open for longer, allowing all the water's ripples and textures to blur and look like glass.

Play around. Don't be afraid to try new things and experiment. Try different shutter speeds to capture movement and different apertures to add a focal point. This is the only way you are going to get to know your camera and create a style that's unique to you.

..........x

Bec Kilpatrick splits her time between the mountains of Canada and the beaches of Australia, chasing photographs of nature in all its many forms. During a trip to Tongariro National Park on New Zealand's North Island, she was reminded that it's worth getting up for sunrises and sticking around for chilly sunsets for the chance to capture images like these.

The call of the waves

....

From his first tentative swim on a boogie board in Australia's southern waters, constantly on the lookout for dangers, to using the ocean as the impetus, inspiration and focus of his lauded magazine *Paper Sea*, Andy Summons has spent his life around the ocean. The sea is endlessly changeable, and its nature is always challenging those who are drawn to it. As long as you keep going back to it, you need to accept the adventure and the risk that is at the heart of any ocean venture. It's a lesson that extends beyond the beach.

My earliest memory of the ocean is from when I was five years old. It was a windy, overcast day, and we were at the back beach in the Australian town of Flinders, Victoria. Everything was grey; I remember the pain of the slicing wind whipping dry sand into my bare legs. The water was a mad squall and tiny, sharp waves prickled the water. The huge dark areas lurking beneath the ocean's surface represented every imaginable fear. Sharks – yep; sea snakes – probably; blue-ringed octopuses – definitely.

The first time I swam over a seaweed patch I held on to my dad's shoulders as he tried to show me there was nothing to fear. After a lot of experimenting and vigilant observation from the safety of a boogie board, I learnt that Dad had been correct. It was the first in a series of ongoing lessons learnt in and from the ocean.

Do you remember that shivering thrill of experiencing something beyond what you thought possible? As a kid, it seemed to happen every day; it probably did. There was so much more to explore, so many firsts and experiences to discover. We had a passion for finding the new – a nervous, ardent determination to step beyond ourselves, just to see what would happen.

As we accrue more confidence, stories and scars, that which once pumped an elixir of terror and excitement through our veins starts to feel safe. And then, after years of exploration and growth, usually for no tangible reason at all, we stop exploring. We grow comfortable with the familiar, unwittingly letting the shivering thrill of tearing through our expectations become a fading memory. An anecdote. A story for the kids.

How often do you slow down and reflect? Think about how and where you're spending your time and energy, and where that's taking you? Writer and historian Will Durant once said, 'We are what we repeatedly do' – so what are you? Think back to that childhood passion for adventure. It hasn't died. It's just been boxed up and stored in the back shed of your head.

Soaring sea levels aside, the ocean has remained fundamentally the same for generations: a sage teacher ready to assist those who are willing to challenge themselves and learn. Each time you go the beach, there are new opportunities to learn and grow. I believe our fascination with the ocean is due to the boundless opportunities it provides for self-exploration and growth. That's why I love the ocean. That's why I will always dedicate time and energy to exploring my relationship with it.

A lifetime of learning from the ocean has helped me in ways I'm still realising. Things I've learnt while surfing and swimming, diving and floating have popped up to help me. The ocean is a vital part of my life and I'm deeply grateful for all that it gives. Even the swiftest ocean swim, the most desperate or frustrating surf, the least bountiful dive and the floppiest bodysurf give me a tectonic shift towards a more positive mental calm.

The ocean provides practically limitless opportunity to challenge ourselves, break through our expectations, reset them and try again. Everything we feel, dream and hope can be found in the ocean. The question is whether or not we are willing to go and search for it.

..........x

> Even the swiftest ocean swim, the most desperate or frustrating surf, the least bountiful dive and the floppiest bodysurf give me a tectonic shift towards a more positive mental calm.

"

Everything we feel, dream and hope can be found in the ocean. The question is whether or not we are willing to go and search for it.

Where the road takes you

When Alexandra Oetzell came home to San Diego after a year of art school in Florence, she found it hard to settle back into life's regular routine: get a job, an apartment, a car. Instead she bought a second-hand, yellow American school bus and converted it into a tiny house complete with bed, table and chairs, and kitchen. Then she drove solo across California and into the states beyond. These days, her time and routines are determined only by the road, the people she meets and her boundless sense of adventure.

What made you decide to leave San Diego behind and live in a bus?

There is kind of an unexplainable feeling you get when you are drawn to a place or an idea. No matter how great my life was in San Diego – all the people in it, the beautiful landscapes and oceans I had – I felt very drawn to the unknown. It's a romantic idea, and a new way to learn about myself. I like to have a very rough plan that will not limit me, so I set out about a year in which to do all of this, and it has been so grand.

What made you pick a bus rather than a van?

I was originally thinking about buying a camper van, but the more research I did, the more converted vehicles I saw. I thought to myself … I can do that, too! I could buy something and make it my own. I chose to get an empty vehicle as a fun and challenging project, and old-school buses were easy to come by. I got my 1987 Ford Econoline – I bought the first one I checked out in person, as I was excited and nervous. I did most of the conversion on my own. I got help with things like taking the seats out and installing a greywater tank underneath. Those were two-person jobs, with heavy lifting and more hands needed.

How long have you been living in the bus now?

I moved out of my apartment and into the bus in the summer of 2016, while I was still living in San Diego. I saved a couple of month's rent that way, just parking around the neighborhood and showering at the gym, the beach or at friends' houses. I left San Diego in mid-August and began my adventure. I drove up through California, Nevada, Idaho,

Wyoming, Colorado, New Mexico, Texas, and now I'm in Louisiana. I plan to head for Florida after my stay here in New Orleans. The plan is to go up the East Coast to New York, then head into Canada.

Does being on the road inspire you to create art?

I am absolutely inspired by the things I see and the people I meet. It's nice to see landscapes, culture and people changing right before your eyes as you're driving. I am not very good about buckling down and making art, especially since I just finished art school and got a little burnt out on art projects. But for every state I pass through, I paint some sort of collage.

How do you feel as a woman travelling solo?

I enjoy spending time by myself. It can get a little lonely if I haven't made any friends on the road after about three days or so, but it's no big deal. I spend lots of time driving anyway. I love catching up on books I've been meaning to read, things I've been meaning to write, or pictures I've been meaning to paint. I love spending time with people, so being isolated leaves me no excuse not to catch up on things I love. I do make lots of friends and have romances while travelling, which is always lovely.

Women travelling solo will always get 'the talk'. From strangers, friends and family: 'Don't go doing this, don't go here, make sure someone is with you'. Usually it's just a reflection of their own fears. It's an important personal decision, figuring out where to draw the line between being adventurous and being reckless. But the world is safer than the news and media make it out to be.

Even before travelling in the bus, I went backpacking in other countries alone. Don't let being solo stop you from going someplace or seeing something. But at the same time, you should always be on your guard and use common sense. Ask for help if you are uncomfortable. Travelling alone is empowering, and I hope all women (and men) get a chance to feel that.

What advice would you give other women thinking of embracing van life?

My absolute best advice is do *not* wait. Don't wait for your best friend or significant other. Go for it! Friends can always join in later; if you want to do it, do it now! Start looking for your 'dream house on wheels'. Worse comes to worst, you get a van and it doesn't work out – you can sell it. It's not a huge commitment. It's a tiny house on wheels that gives you the absolute freedom to go anywhere. Dive in headfirst; you can always backtrack a little.

Van life gives you a chance to get to know yourself so much better. After that first week, you overcome the fear and nerves that come with sleeping in it alone. Downsizing clothes and furniture might be tough at first, but it helps you separate needs from wants. When you die, you're taking nothing physical with you. Make some memories and have less stuff: it's pure bliss. The van is just a tool to help you obtain freedom.

Where do you go to reconnect with nature?

I feel really connected with nature when camping in the bus in the country or at national parks. I've heard wolves howling outside my window. I love being parked by the beach or a lake: being able to take a dip in the morning, then go back to the bus to dry off and make some coffee. I feel connected to nature when I wake up to the sun peeking through the curtains, or when I see a beautiful sunrise over the mountains or lake. I like to put my chair outside, or sit on the roof, or swing the back doors wide open to the world and have a snack, and just spend some time taking it all in. I'm happy to step outside my comfort zone with the bus; it helps take me there.

..........x

"

When you die, you're taking nothing physical with you. Make some memories and have less stuff: it's pure bliss.

What's washed ashore

James Herman grew up in Oregon in the United States, but it wasn't until he reached his twenties that he stumbled across the coast's driftwood forts. These ad-hoc, temporary structures are forts of all kinds, from teepees to shacks, made from the driftwood that washes up on the beach. They are a local tradition built for shelter from the wind, to protect campfires, or simply for the pleasure of building.

Driftwood forts represent the hardy self-build culture of the Pacific Northwest, a theme explored in manifestos like Lloyd Kahn's *Shelter* and the *Whole Earth Catalog*. James devoured these books growing up, and his art has increasingly revolved around self-building. He documented these forts through photos and by recording lists of the materials they contained, eventually posting them online. For James, this isn't just about art; it's also a paean to self-build culture, which he continued to explore when he and his friends built a studio on a property in Los Angeles, surrounded by fruit trees and land he happily tends.

How did your interest in driftwood forts begin?

I was walking down the beach in Lincoln City, Oregon, where I was doing an artist residency. I would routinely walk the beach in search of shells, agates, driftwood, rocks and other things to take with me to the studio. One day, there they were: grey, tall masses of wood pointing everywhere, built with pieces of driftwood or other debris that had washed ashore. I'd never seen the forts before in my life. Some of them held remnants of fires from the night before, where children sat and watched their parents dig for clams. Some fires were still burning.

They consumed me for the rest of my time at the residency. I searched miles and miles of beach for them.

Can you tell us a bit about your work surrounding driftwood forts?

There's this film, *The Subconscious Art of Graffiti Removal*, which takes a tongue-in-cheek look at graffiti removal. The film cleverly elevates the status of the people who paint over graffiti into high art. I thought, 'What if I could elevate driftwood sculptures in a similar way?' That's why I began documenting the materials used in the forts I found, as if I were writing an art book. But the project evolved into something different – social, too, with a website and an Instagram account. Pictures of forts have been sent in from Japan, New Zealand, Australia and the United States.

> "
> I'd never seen the forts before in my life. Some of them held remnants of fires from the night before, where children sat and watched their parents dig for clams. Some fires were still burning.

How did you first hear about the self-build culture?

In college I found out about the *Whole Earth Catalog*, which blew my mind. I was fascinated with the back-to-the-land movement, domes, yurts and the hippie lifestyle. I wanted to recreate that for myself.

What do you like about self-building?

I think starting from scratch, with limitless options, is possibly the most lifeless and boring way to build. My approach is to find something you love and make a plan based off of that. There's no way you're going to be bummed about what you make when you put all that intention and consideration into building around or incorporating that special thing.

How has your work in self-building evolved since you first started documenting driftwood forts?

I first started documenting forts and writing about the process in 2012. Later that year I moved to Los Angeles from Oregon to better establish myself in the art world. By 2014 I was living in a small duplex in the Lincoln Heights neighbourhood, tucked behind a larger house. I began to realise I needed a change. I often walked up the hill at the end of my street to a sort of no-man's-land, a series of mostly vacant lots with incredible views of the city. That was there I met Paige, who gave me the freedom and space to build a studio and convert an outbuilding on her property into a small house. It's a vast property, almost half a hectare (an acre): twenty or thirty fruit trees, doves in a giant walk-in aviary, chickens, quails, and now turkeys and a tortoise. It also has two non-adjoining structures, each about 18.5 square metres (200 square feet) in size. I saw the run-down state of the structures and how badly the trees needed care as the opportunity of a lifetime. I began building myself into the fabric of the place.

Are you trying to create a physical community around your self-build work in LA?

On my birthday, I hosted what was more or less a barn raising. Instead of having all my friends meet somewhere like a bar, we met at the site of what is now my studio and worked together to fix it up. I was initially shy about hosting something that would most definitely be benefitting me, but my friends assured me that the people helping would get something out of it, too – a shared sense of accomplishment. So we cleaned the site, put the roof on my studio, and ate and drank all day. I highly recommend this sort of activity, and I am hoping to host more of them for other friends. We can all help each other on the road to the next big thing.

How do you connect with nature in your day-to-day life?

Most days I'm tending to the trees or plants in some way. I feel more connected to nature here. The hillside is always buzzing with life, between the birds, squirrels and coyotes. I walk, run and hike throughout the week. I'm lucky to live where I do.

..........x

> "
> I saw the run-down state of the structures and how badly the trees needed care as the opportunity of a lifetime. I began building myself into the fabric of the place.

HOW TO PLAN FOR A CAR CAMPING TRIP

One of the many joys of camping with transport, whether that's a four-wheel-drive setup, camper van or just a car, is that it lets you set up a fully functional and comfortable campsite. Lightweight camping is great, but there's nothing like a camp out in nature with a few home comforts to make it that much more enjoyable. It encourages you to stay awhile and tune in to your surroundings. It allows you to take along items you would never consider on a lightweight adventure: a large tent, a comfortable mattress, a cool box, a camp kitchen, cast-iron cooking gear – maybe even a camp shower. Let these tips guide you to car camping greatness.

Research destinations and routes before you leave. The internet can be a fount of great information, but local knowledge and in-the-know friends are the best resources for finding 'The Spot'.

Check to see what sort of road leads in to the campsite and if your car can handle the conditions. Make sure to check whether you can drive your car up to the campsite too – otherwise you'll have to carry your gear in.

Check conditions: you'll want to be prepared for both the weather and the environment you will be camping in. Arrive well before sundown – the earlier the better, to avoid setting up camp in the dark.

Create a checklist of the essentials and non-essentials you want to take (see opposite page).

Get to know your gear before heading off. Set up your tent at least once before departing. Note the best way to pack and unpack it, and ensure all poles and pegs are safely stowed. Don't forget to pack your mallet!

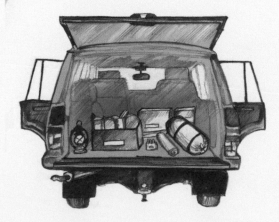

Plan your meals and, if possible, prep as much food as possible beforehand. Pack food into resealable plastic bags or portable containers – even better, use a vacuum sealer (a worthwhile investment). Pack the dry food into one large container and put everything that needs to stay cool in a cool box. Take a second cool box for beverages so you can get to everything easily. It's a good idea to pack things in the cool box in the order you'll need them. Test your stove before you leave.

Organise your gear into large, clear plastic tubs that fit snugly into your car's trunk – again, it's a good idea to pack things in the order you'll need them. Fill up a tub with your kitchen gear and pack separate tubs for lighting equipment, such as lanterns and matches, and washing up. Once you're done with packing, label your tubs. Use a utensil/tool roll to protect knives and a multi-compartment plastic toolbox for other handy bits like bottle openers, tools and rubber bands. Large tote bags are also a good idea, as they are easy to access and carry.

Take a spare set of car keys and keep them somewhere safe, along with an extra torch (flashlight). Leave an extra lighter in your glovebox to make sure it stays dry.

Pack your vehicle systematically so that you can access essentials like your tent, lighting and wet weather gear easily as you start to unpack.

HOW TO PACK FOR A CAR CAMPING TRIP

Camping may be one of the best ways to connect with nature, but it requires foresight and planning – and a good checklist. This list will help ensure that you have a comfortable campsite and that you leave no trace of your visit behind.

Shelter, sleeping and relaxing

- Tent (double check you have your poles, pegs, guylines and spares)
- Mallet with a heavy, metal head
- Sleeping pads like the Exped MegaMat or an inflatable mattress
- Sleeping bag, blankets and/or a doona (comforter)
- Pillows
- Headlamps and a torch (flashlight), as well as extra batteries
- Camp chairs and a foldable, lightweight table
- Lanterns, such as a kerosene storm lantern and a battery lantern
- Hard-wearing picnic rug and blankets

Cooking and the fire

- Stove and fuel
- Two cool boxes (one for beverages and one for food) and ice
- Drinking water and an easy-to-fill container for collecting water onsite
- Water filter or treatment tablets
- Funnel
- Lighters and matches (stored in waterproof containers)
- Charcoal (with firestarter)
- Firewood and kindling (always check to see if you are allowed to collect wood at the site)
- Frying pan (a 25.5 cm/10 in pan is ideal)

- Favourite camp coffee-making device, like an Aeropress (see *How to make the perfect campfire brew* on page 252)
- Cooking pots (don't take your favourites; get camping pots from a second-hand store)
- Plates, bowls, mixing bowls and mugs (bamboo, BPA-free plastics or enamel are a good investment)
- Utensils such as a chef/chopping knife, paring knife, serving spoon, cutlery and long metal skewers, and a utensil roll for safely transporting them
- Barbecue spatula and fork
- Chopping board
- Cooking oil or spray
- Condiments, salt and pepper
- Foil and plastic wrap
- Vacuum bottle/thermos
- Water bottles
- Tupperware or airtight food containers
- Resealable plastic storage bags
- Rubbish bags

Useful tools

- Fixed-blade knife (this needs to be sharp and in its sheath when not in use)
- Saw or axe/hatchet (folding saws are a very handy camp tool for cutting wood for fuel – see *How to chop firewood* on page 244)
- Foldable shovel with sharp blade (great for digging out car wheels, creating a fire pit, tending the fire or digging a latrine)
- Multi-tool or Swiss Army knife that includes a knife, bottle opener, corkscrew and can opener
- Gaffer tape
- Rope or paracord (some of its many uses include washing line and tarp ridgelines)
- Carabiners and adjustable webbing straps (you will find many uses for these)

Washing up and cleaning

- Collapsible washing-up tub
- Biodegradable soap
- Steel scrubs and sponges
- Collapsible water container(s)
- Kitchen towels
- Tea towels
- Dust pan and brush (helpful for keeping the tent free of dirt)
- Bucket with lid

Personal

- Toiletry bag with common-sense essentials
- Baby wipes and hand sanitiser
- Toilet paper in a resealable plastic bag
- Sunscreen, lip balm and insect repellent
- Towels

Miscellaneous

- Luggage (backpacks, tote bags, duffels and other soft bags are a good idea)
- Daypack

- Spare clothing, particularly for warmth (jackets, hoodies, beanie, shorts, socks, thermals, fleece, merino underwear, swimming gear – you never know how cold or wet things will get)
- Wet-weather gear
- Sun hat or cap with detachable mosquito/fly net
- Hiking boots or trail shoes
- Thongs (flip flops)
- Gloves (fingerless is a great way to stay warm and still accomplish things around camp)
- Maps and a compass
- Spare car key kept in a safe place
- Spare batteries and extra fuel for lantern(s) and stove
- Sunglasses
- Spare eyeglasses and contact lenses
- First aid kit with whistle, painkillers and rehydration packs
- Watch with an alarm

Not essential, but nice to have

- Griddle or grill rack for cooking on an open fire
- Shade tarp
- Hammock
- Mosquito/fly netting
- Dutch oven
- Camera
- Umbrella
- Binoculars
- Solar powered batteries (check out Goal Zero)
- Trekking poles
- Two-way radio set
- Bluetooth speaker (waterproof)
- Biking/kayaking/fishing gear

HOW TO CHOOSE A CAMPSITE

When it comes to picking your spot, learning what to look for and what to steer clear of is a crucial part of enjoying the experience. First, you need to figure out what kind of camping you're doing: established campground camping with facilities or a more remote adventure? From there, it's all about protection from the elements and a nice, flat piece of land.

If you've only camped one or two times before, plan to stay in an established campground. These will usually have amenities such as a designated fire pit, a picnic table and flushing toilets (sometimes even a shower). Try not to camp too close to the bathroom facilities, as they attract heavy traffic and produce strong odours – a site at least a short walk away will provide a much needed olfactory buffer zone.

For more experienced campers, a remote location or bush camp will give you more opportunities for seclusion and are the best way to experience nature's ambiance. It's best, however, to choose an established campsite in an official camping area so that you can minimise your impact on the landscape you've come so far to enjoy.

If you're out in the wild, choose a campsite near a river or other water source. Apart from giving you access to fresh drinking water (make sure you boil it first!), you'll also have a place to bathe (although you shouldn't use soap in rivers and lakes) and a water source for washing up, cooking and dousing fires. If you've got kids with you, be mindful of fast-flowing water.

Avoid camping in old riverbeds or gullies. Instead, look for a level piece of ground near a slope so water can run off in the event of rain. Think about the position of the sun and shade – the morning sun will dry a canvas tent, and ideally you'll want shade from the midday sun. However much you want shade, avoid camping under a tree – falling branches, critters and insects can make this hazardous.

Finally, choose a spot that is sheltered from prevailing winds. Remember, you can use your vehicle as shade or wind protection if you need it.

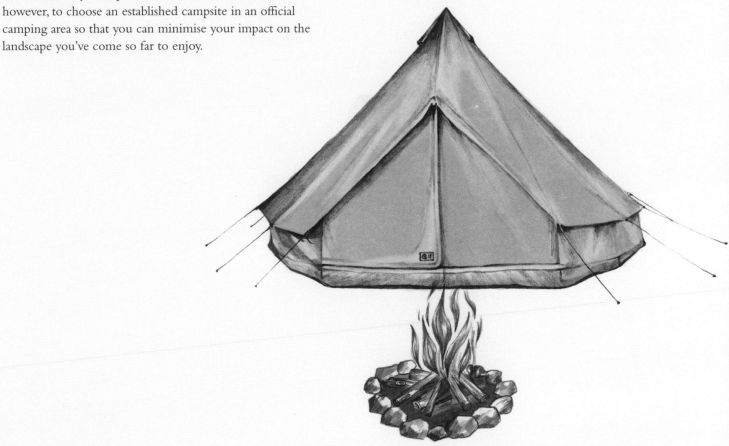

HOW TO SET UP A CAMPSITE

Organising your campsite is key to having a relaxed experience. Once it gets dark, you don't want to have to stumble around, tripping over random piles of equipment while you search in vain for this pot or that blanket. Camping is best enjoyed when everything has its designated place and is easy to lay your hands on when you need it.

The first thing to do after arriving at a campsite is set up your shelter and kitchen areas. Plan these spaces by laying your gear out on the ground. Try to keep your cooking, eating and washing up areas well away from your tent.

Choose a flat spot on which to pitch your tent (see *How to choose a campsite* on page 241). Remove any debris, such as rocks or sticks, that could damage your groundsheet or make for an uncomfortable stay. Pace out the size of your tent, making sure you have plenty of room on all sides for the guyropes.

Camping in the wild instead of in designated campgrounds might mean you have to build your own latrine area. Make sure this area is well away from your camp. Be mindful about hygiene and any potential water contamination issues. Most importantly, leave no trace – that means no toilet paper chucked in the latrine.

A fire pit is an essential for the full camping experience. Cooking on an open fire is one of life's great culinary experiences, and the campfire will be your main source of light and heat. If possible, use an existing fire circle that past campers have left behind. If you need to make one from scratch, choose an area of about 3 m (10 ft) in diameter that is free of flammable debris and grass – bare soil, sand or gravel is best. If you have a camp shovel, dig out a shallow circle, about 1 m (3 ft) wide, and place rocks around the circumference of your pit to ensure your fire doesn't spread (see *How to build a campfire* on page 246).

Keep your camp tidy to cut down on animals in your campsite and prevent you from tripping over things in the dark. You and your campmates should strive to develop good camp routines and habits, like washing up after eating and returning tools and equipment to their designated space. Keep all food and food waste in sealed containers that critters and insects can't access. If your campsite has bear boxes or other storage containers on site, use them.

If you foraged for your wood (see *How to chop firewood* on page 244), keep it handy in a designated area. Remember that freshly cut wood often needs to dry out. Proximity to the fire will help with this process, but be mindful that it can ignite if you're not careful.

Always put your fire out before going to sleep or leaving your site (see *How to build a campfire* on page 246).

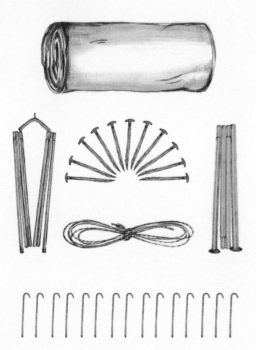

HOW TO TIE USEFUL CAMPING KNOTS

You don't have to know these simple knots to go camping, but they will prove helpful when it comes to everything from making sure your tent is securely anchored to stringing up a hammock. These classics have withstood the test of time and are very useful for a simple camping setup.

Bowline knot

The bowline knot, otherwise known as 'The King of Knots', is a classic fixed-loop knot used to secure an object to something else – whether that's securing a tarp or a hammock to a tree, or hanging up your food/kitchen gear where camp critters can't reach it. The bowline is particularly popular because it tightens under weight, doesn't slip and, when not supporting weight, is easy to tie and untie. It's a simple knot to learn, particularly if you memorise this well-known mnemonic: 'up through the rabbit hole, around the big tree; down through the rabbit hole and off goes he'.

Square (reef) knot

A good choice for joining two ropes of equal weight and thickness together, the square knot can be used to tie a bundle of kindling or secure rubbish bags. This knot is not suitable for supporting anything weighty (like a human) and will slip under tension.

  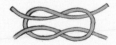

Tautline hitch

The tautline hitch is a supremely clever knot, useful for securing tent or tarp guylines to pegs. It creates tension between the tent and the peg; when the tautline hitch has been tied correctly, it's easy to adjust the tension back and forth.

 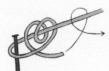 

Timber hitch

The timber hitch is used to attach a length of rope to a cylindrical object such as a log. It's often used by arborists or woodsmen to drag or tow a bundle of logs, as it will tighten with strain and lets go easily when that strain eases.

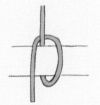 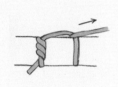

Double half (clove) hitch

This is a practical, easy-to-learn knot whose main function is securing a rope directly to an object, often a branch, log or post. The double half hitch can be used to tether animals or secure a tarp or hammock, but it can slip if it isn't under enough tension.

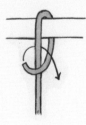  

HOW TO CHOP FIREWOOD

There's something satisfying, almost primeval, about swinging an axe and splitting a log, about feeling the rasp of the wood against your palm and splinters in your fingers as you pile the chopped wood high ready for seasoning. It's an achievement, being ready for winter, knowing you'll be able to sit around a roaring home or campfire, feeding it log after log, as you share meals and stories around its warmth.

You will need:
good-quality axe
chopping block (or tree stump)
sturdy footwear
logs

Collecting wood

Before collecting wood, you need to know the rules in the area where you're camping. Chopping down a tree or picking up fallen branches isn't always legal, particularly in national parks. If you find yourself in need of a regular supply of wood, we recommend making friends with your local arborist. They can also give you guidance on which type of wood is best for fires both indoors and out.

Preparing your logs

Once you've collected your wood, you may need to chop it into smaller logs or 'rounds' – in other words, break it down into smaller pieces that will be easier to split (not pictured). Your logs need to be short enough to fit into a fire pit or wood stove. You'll also want to even out the ends of each log so that it can stand up straight – a necessity for chopping wood.

Positioning your logs

Place the log on top of your chopping block – this can be a handy tree stump or a larger log – and make sure the log is standing up straight. It's harder to chop logs with knots or irregularities towards the bottom, as the grain around these knots will be tougher to split.

Holding your axe

Chopping wood isn't about strength and muscle – it's all about using the axe to your advantage and letting it do the work for you.

Take your axe in both hands, with your dominant hand near the head of the axe and your nondominant hand near the end of the handle. As you swing the axe, let your dominant hand slide down the handle to meet your other hand for the greatest accuracy and power.

Taking a swing

Take a steady, square stance in front of your chopping block. Line up your axe with where you want it to strike – aim for small cracks already present in the wood for easier splitting. Once lined up, bring the axe up over your head and swing down quickly and firmly.

Chopping to size

Depending on the size of your logs, you may need to split them in half or into quarters. After splitting in half, reposition one half of your log on the chopping block and split that in half. Repeat with the other half of the log.

Stacking and seasoning

If you're cutting firewood for at-home use, you want to stack it where it will be protected from the elements, but also where the sun will dry the moisture from the logs – this process is called seasoning. Ideally you want to cut, split and stack your firewood in early spring to give it time to fully season. Depending on your location and climate, this could take anywhere from six months to a year. If you're in a rainy area, cover your firewood a few weeks before you plan to use it.

If you don't have time to wait for the wood to dry, make a hot fire of dry wood and kindling and add the unseasoned logs once the fire is well established.

Positioning your logs

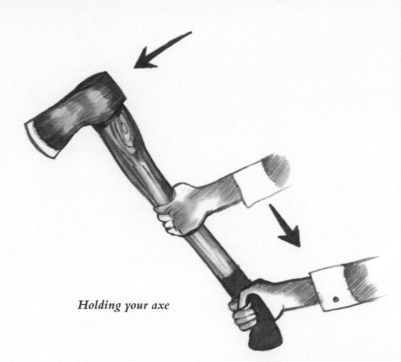

Holding your axe

Taking a swing

Stacking and seasoning

HOW TO BUILD A CAMPFIRE

A roaring campfire is essential when you're spending a night in the bush. It does more than ward off the dark and any inquisitive animals; it's the heart of the campsite. The place where you'll gather to stay warm, cook and swap stories long into the night, until the fire is nothing more than smouldering embers.

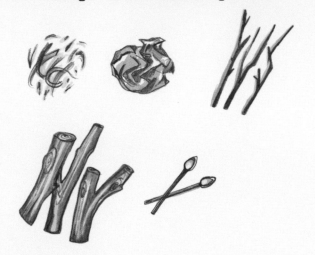

You will need:
shovel (for digging your fire pit and moving hot coals)
newspaper and woodchips
kindling (thin twigs and branches around the length
  of a drinking straw)
tinder (light, dry fuel such as bark and woodchips)
fuelwood (thicker branches, preferably dead fallen logs)
matches

Picking the fire's location
You'll need to set up your fire well before dark so you can see what you're doing, a process that starts by selecting your campfire's location. Most campsites will have fire pits or cleared patches of ground where others have set up campfires. If you have to create your own, choose the location carefully; it should be clear of anything that might catch (like brush or dry grass) and have no overhanging branches. Dig a hole around 10 cm (4 in) deep and 1 m (3 ft) wide and surround it with a wide circle of rocks to keep the fire from spreading.

Preparing your tinder and kindling
Place loosely scrunched newspaper and tinder in the centre of the fire pit. When foraging for tinder, look for soft wood, dry bark, small twigs, pinecones or pine needles. You could

use a sharp knife to pare fine strips of softwood or shred the bark (see *How to chop firewood* on page 244). Make sure your tinder is dry or you'll get a fire that smokes a lot and not much else.

Lodge one thick stick into the ground at the centre of your fire. Lean your kindling in a loose teepee shape against it, around the pile of tinder.

Lighting your fire
Light the paper and tinder in a few places around the teepee. Gradually add more kindling, placing it using the same teepee formation as before. Blow on the base of the fire to add oxygen and build the flames. Once your fire is crackling merrily, add the fuelwood around the base of the teepee. Don't add the fuelwood too quickly, as this can smother the fire – start with two logs on opposite sides of the fire and build up.

Putting out your fire
Let your fire burn down to ashes before gently dousing it with water; the fire may hiss and smoke, so don't stand too close. Keep pouring water onto the fire until the hissing stops. Mix the embers together with a shovel until everything is wet. Once everything is wet, reach in and feel the ashes. They should be cold to the touch. Pick up the rocks on the edge of your fire circle and feel the ground underneath. If anything still feels warm, you need to continue watering the fire. Once your fire is doused to your satisfaction, scour the surrounding ground for any embers or sparks. If water is in short supply, bury the remains of your fire with dirt or sand.

HOW TO SPIT ROAST

Slowly cooking a joint of meat over an open fire is, for some, the pinnacle of primitive camp cooking. Using a portable spit roaster – or better yet, a spit you have fashioned from a hardwood branch – is a sure-fire way to impress your fellow campers. The slowly turning meat will self-baste, resulting in a sweetly charred, succulent roast that's full of flavour.

Building the spit

Take some fresh green wood from a nearby tree to make your single-use spit roast. Look for a branch from a hardwood tree – you are looking for a straight piece with a kink at one end, which will become the 'crank' of the spit. Choose one about 3 cm (1 in) thick; the ideal length will depend on the size of your cut of meat.

Using a sharp hunting knife, hatchet or machete, remove the side branches and pare off the bark. Sharpen the end (the one without the crank) to a point.

Supporting the spit

Find two strong branches with Y forks at one end, which will be what supports your spit. These branches will ideally be at least 25 cm (10 in) from the foot to the fork, and at least 3 cm (1 in) thick.

Remove the bark from both sticks and sharpen the foot ends to a point.

Using a mallet, drive the supporting forks into the earth at the appropriate distance to leave about 10 cm (4 in) of your spit at each end.

You will need:

1 butterflied lamb, rolled boneless beef, tenderloin roast, rolled pork loin, whole chicken or rabbit (1.5 to 2 kg/3½ to 4½ lb)

2 garlic cloves, finely chopped or crushed

handful of fresh herbs such as rosemary and sage, chopped or crushed

zest of one lemon

1 tsp sea salt

freshly ground black pepper

4 tbsp olive oil

If you are feeding a lot of people, you might use the whole animal – lamb or pig are a good bet. You will need to adjust the size of your spit accordingly.

Preparing the meat

Bring the meat to room temperature. Place it in a plastic bag or mixing bowl. In a separate bowl, mix the garlic, herbs, lemon zest, salt, pepper and oil. Add half of this mixture to the bag or mixing bowl with the meat, ensuring it is evenly covered.

Using the sharp end of the spit, penetrate the meat lengthwise from end to end. You might want to use a skewer or two to ensure the meat is secured to the spit. If you are roasting a rolled beef or butterflied lamb, then use cooking twine to hold it together.

Cooking the meat

About an hour before you start cooking, build a fire near your spit setup. Make sure your fire is producing plenty of hot coals before you start cooking your meat.

Attach your meat spit to the supporting Y forks – your spit should be about 15 cm (6 in) away from the coalbed.

Place a cast-iron pan filled with generous splashes of water and wine beneath your meat – it will collect the meat's drippings to make gravy later and help prevent fire flare-ups.

Using your shovel, start to build a hot coalbed around the dripping pan and between the supporting forks. You will start to notice your meat sizzling slowly. As it starts to change colour, use the crank to turn it every now and again. Baste the meat occasionally with the remainder of your herb marinade.

Here's a tip: it's a good idea to maintain your main fire so that you have a steady supply of hot coals at hand. You can control the pace of your cooking by moving your coalbed towards or away from the meat.

Cooking time will depend on the size and type of your meat cut, but expect to cook for at least an hour – the slower, the better. Watch your campmates melt with anticipation as the meat nears cooked perfection. Serve with fire-roasted veggies, gravy and a good beverage.

HOW TO COOK ON AN OPEN FIRE

There are many ways to cook on an open fire. With a minimum of tools – all you really need is a stick – you can hold food at the optimum distance from heat in order to crisp or roast it. As you expand your culinary range, include stews, casseroles and fry-ups, or increase the size of your portions with larger cuts of meat, you will need to invest in some tools and utensils to manage open-fire cooking.

Equipment to use over open flames

Pots, skillets and saucepans: Cast-iron is our preference for cooking on an open fire, as it's durable, heats evenly and can handle extreme temperatures. Cast-iron is heavy, though, so its not recommended for lightweight camping adventures.

Dutch (camp) ovens: A Dutch oven is a large pot with a lid and legs. The best ones are made of cast-iron and may well be the only camp cookware you will ever need. The advantage of a Dutch oven is its versatility; you can reproduce just about any one-pot dish that you could make at home on your kitchen stove. Dutch ovens retain and distribute heat evenly, which means less chance of burning your food. It offers a tremendous amount of control with cooking, as you can cover the oven with coals or move it further away from the heat source when needed.

Grills and griddle plates: A grill is a metal grate that will support your food at the right distance from the coal bed. Having a stable, flat surface is handy for pots, pans and kettles. You can adjust the height of the grill or move the coals into different layers beneath the grill to control the heat. Griddle plates are great for cooking smaller pieces of meat (rashers, chops, chicken) or veggies without them falling through into the fire.

Other bits of useful camp cooking kit

Fireproof mitts or gloves: Getting close to hot fires can easily lead to burns. A pair of fireproof mitts or gloves are essential for safe campfire cooking.

Long-handled spoon or fork: Used to prod food, remove lids from pots and move coals around the fire.

Shovel: Used for digging a fire pit and moving hot coals around.

Building a fire hot enough for roasting

Build and light your fire (see *How to build a campfire* on page 246). When building a fire to roast food, it pays to have some hardwood on hand. Hardwood is the best fuel for producing extremely hot coals, which will be crucial for roasting and grilling. Try to have your hardwood chopped to kindling size, as smaller pieces of wood will burn down to coals more quickly (see *How to chop firewood* on page 244). Building a second, and even a third, fire with kindling tipis is a great way to get your cooking fire producing coal quickly.

After your fire has burnt for about half an hour, the flames will start reducing and your fire will begin producing hot coals. These will give off an even heat, which you can control by moving around your cookware, spit or grill. At this stage, you will need to be vigilant about continuing to stoke the fire's heat with fresh fuel.

Using a long-handled spoon or shovel, you can isolate the hot coals and move them to the side that will become your cooking fire. You can keep adding more kindling to the main fire, as this will keep producing hot coals for your cooking fire.

You now have the option of either cooking directly on the coals, using a pot or skillet, or setting up a grill, or even a spit.

Roasting some veggies

Some vegetables are perfect for roasting in a campfire with little or no preparation or tools. You can simply bury veggies such as potatoes, sweet potatoes, butternut pumpkin (squash), Jerusalem artichokes, turnips, chestnuts, garlic and onions in the hot ashes, or set them near hot coals, for an hour or so. When you retrieve your treasure from the fire, simply peel away the outer layer or slice the veggie in half and spoon out its soft centre. If you want to keep the skin of your veggie intact, then wrap it in aluminium foil prior to cooking or, better yet, in soaked banana or palm leaves.

To roast corn ears, soak them in water for an hour, then place directly onto your hot coals. Cook for 30 minutes or so, turning a few times, and you will be rewarded with wonderfully charred husks and perfectly steamed corn. Just add butter, salt and pepper to achieve instant camp legend status.

If you want to get a little fancy, you can't beat Hasselback potatoes: crispy outer layers and beautifully soft, creamy centres make these a campfire favourite. Choose medium-sized roasting spuds. One by one, nestle the potatoes in the curve of a large wooden spoon. Using a sharp knife, slice downwards until your knife hits the edge of the spoon. Work the knife from one end of the potato to the other, spacing your slices about ½ cm (⅛ in) apart. Meanwhile, heat some oil and butter in a pan along with some thin slices of garlic. Brush your potatoes with the oil/butter/garlic mixture, then salt generously. Either wrap your spuds in foil or banana leaves, or arrange in your favourite cookware – a Dutch oven is great for this. You can add grated cheese and chives at the end for extra points.

HOW TO BAKE CAMPFIRE SODA BREAD IN A DUTCH OVEN

There's nothing quite as satisfying or simple as making soda bread over a crackling campfire. This classic Irish bread is known as damper in Australia and a bannock in Scotland – it tastes delicious wherever you make it (and whatever you call it). This recipe has few ingredients and very little preparation, yet will impress your fellow campers no end.

You will need:

3 cups flour (we use a combination of organic wholemeal and white flour – feel free to experiment)

1 tsp salt

1 level tsp bicarbonate of soda (baking soda)

1 cup buttermilk (or 1 cup milk mixed with 1 tbsp lemon juice)

100 g (3½ oz) butter, cold

3 tbsp honey

Optional add-ins:

⅓ cup mixed grain and seed blend, mixed in after you've blended the wet and dry ingredients: sunflower seeds, millet, pumpkin seeds, rolled oats, etc, to add some texture

¾ cup sourdough starter, added to the wet mix for a healthy, fermented bread

replace the buttermilk with probiotic yoghurt or even dark stout

Preparing the dough

Thoroughly combine flours, bicarbonate of soda and salt in a large bowl. We sieve these ingredients together at home and take them camping in a resealable plastic bag or container.

Put the buttermilk in a medium bowl. In a small pan, warm the butter by the fire until soft, then pour it into the buttermilk. Stir in the honey and mix everything together until well combined.

Make a well in the centre of the dry flour mix and slowly pour the wet mix into it. Stir with a wooden spoon for about a minute until the mixture comes together – stir steadily, but not vigorously. If the mix is too dry to form a dough, add a tablespoon or two of milk or water.

Spoon the mix onto a lightly floured surface, such as a chopping board, then knead the dough with floured hands until you achieve a soft and almost fluffy texture. Don't overdo the kneading – just four or five kneads should be enough. The bi-carb soda and buttermilk will react as soon as they meet, and minimal handling will help preserve this reaction. The idea is to get the bread into the Dutch oven while that reaction is still going strong, which means as quickly as possible.

Shape the mixture into a ball, then flatten slightly using the palm of your hand.

Dip a knife in flour and make a deep cross through the centre of the bread, extending each line out to the dough's edges. This will make it easy to break the bread into quarters after it is baked.

Prepping the fire and Dutch oven

The key to cooking bread in a Dutch oven is getting a consistent temperature around the whole pot (see *How to cook on an open fire* on page 248). Make sure your campfire includes plenty of hardwood that had been burning long enough to produce a good number of hot coals.

Using a kitchen towel or newspaper, wipe the inside of your Dutch oven with a thin coating of oil or butter, then dust with flour.

Preheat the Dutch oven by placing it directly on the bed of hot coals. Nestle the ball of dough in the centre of the oven. Put the lid on the pot, making sure no steam is escaping. Push the Dutch oven down into the bed of coals, then use a shovel to cover the lid with coals and embers. You may need to repeat this process during the bake.

Baking and finishing

Bake until the crust is golden brown. The cooking time depends on how hot your coals are, but it generally takes 25 to 35 minutes. To see if your bread is baked, push a knife into the middle of the loaf; if the knife comes out clean, then the bread is done. If the knife comes out wet, with some bread dough sticking to it, then it needs more time. When done, it will also sound hollow when tapped underneath. This bread tastes great even if it's a little under- or overdone, so you don't need to worry about the bake being perfect.

Remove the bread from the oven, brush the top with butter and let it cool under a moist tea towel. Eat as soon as possible with a hearty meal.

HOW TO MAKE THE PERFECT CAMPFIRE BREW

The familiar process of preparing coffee in the morning increases in significance when it happens in the outdoors. The whole process is warming, comforting. The resulting cup of coffee – cradled in your hands as you watch the sunrise – is so much more satisfying. This method for preparing a campfire coffee uses the easily transportable Aeropress, which produces the perfect filter brew.

You will need:
½ litre (17 fl oz) water
Aeropress with filter
fresh coffee beans
coffee grinder
digital scale
timer

Prepping your coffee
Bring at least half a litre (17 fl oz) of fresh water to a boil over the campfire. While you're waiting for the water to boil, measure out 15 g (½ oz) of coffee and grind it to the consistency of table salt or course sand.

Rinse the Aeropress chamber and the filter with the hot water, and warm up your cup with the hot water while you're at it. Save 200 g (7 oz) of hot water for making your coffee. Discard the water from your chamber and filter once you're done.

Setting up your Aeropress
Assemble your Aeropress by pushing the plunger, seal first, slightly into the chamber at the opposite end to where you'll twist on the filter cap. Place your scale on a flat and steady surface, then place the Aeropress on top with the plunger section on the bottom. Add your ground coffee to the top of the seal in the chamber. Tare your scales to zero.

Starting your brew
Add 200 g (7 oz) of boiling water to the ground coffee and start your timer. After one minute, give the brew a good stir. Let it steep for another minute. Place your filter into the filter cap, then attach it to the top of the chamber and twist it in.

Flipping your brew
Place your cup over the filter cap. Very carefully, turn the Aeropress upside down so your cup is now on the scale (or another bit of steady, flat ground).

Filtering your brew
Gently and slowly press the plunger down until the brew is completely pushed through the paper filter. Sit back and enjoy.

Setting up your Aeropress

Starting your brew

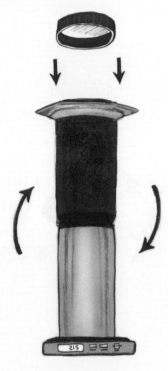

Flipping your brew

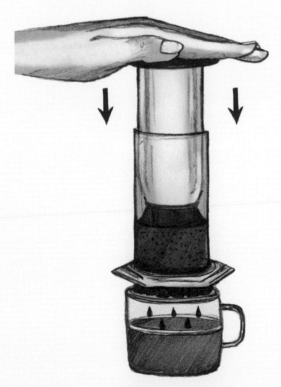

Filtering your brew

Enjoy!

HOW (AND WHY) TO FORAGE FOR SEAWEED

Picking and using wild plants, particularly wild mushrooms, is something that needs to be learnt carefully. Many wild plants are poisonous, some deadly. People worry, and who can blame them? But seaweeds are a different matter. Many are too slimy, too chalky, too small, too tough to eat – or simply just don't taste very good – but none are poisonous. Far Eastern cuisine has long embraced seaweed, but cultures with European origins have all but ignored them.

That seaweeds are nutritious is well known, but besides their high levels of minerals and vitamins, many people don't necessarily realise that they are very high in proteins and amino acids as well. The flavour? Okay, you might have me here. The taste is very much of the sea: unusual, but mild. It's a taste that needs to be acquired, but doing so is not an onerous task such as, say, learning to like the taste of beetroot. I eat seaweed nearly every day, partly for its powerful nutritional properties, but also for its ability to make other foods taste better. Seaweeds are high in glutamates and umami flavours, so they can easily enhance any savoury dish.

The problem with seaweeds is that they simply do not *look* very edible, and there is nothing particularly obvious that can be cooked with them. The average home cook with a bucket of the best edible seaweed would probably not know where to start and have little inclination to try. Yet seaweed is easy to collect, provided your coast is tidal and the seaweeds exposed at least once a day.

The twenty or so seaweeds that are considered the best for eating tend to need their own special cooking method. Laver (*Porphyra umbilicalis*), which is common on the Irish and Welsh coasts lining the Irish Sea, must either be boiled for around 10 hours into a sticky paste called laverbread, or made into the toasted nori sheet we know from sushi rolls (it is also found in Asia). Kelps, which are found all over the world, are seldom eaten directly – they are used instead to give a dish flavour before being discarded, similar to bay leaves. Carrageen (*Chondrus crispus*), sometimes called Irish moss, is found everywhere from Europe to America and Australasia and is employed solely for the complex carbohydrates it contains, which help set milk-based dishes like pannacotta. Dulse (*Palmaria palmata*) is the most versatile of seaweeds, and the one most like an 'ordinary' vegetable in that it can be fried, boiled, steamed or sautéed. The cook must simply learn these techniques and experiment to find the method that works best for them.

Dulse is my favourite seaweed; tasty, high in protein, easy to find and prepare. I wash and dry it first on a canvas sheet in the garden, then cook it to crispness in an oven on low heat. Once the seaweed is crisp, I reduce it to a fine powder in a blender. I add this to just about anything, but it's particularly terrific when sprinkled on scallops or white fish. And it's a sure way to impress your dinner guests.

John Wright, who shared the recipes above and at right, is a forager who lives in England. He shares his skills and knowledge of foraging in the coast and the forest sustainably, often through his work with River Cottage, an organisation that promotes healthy eating and sustainable agriculture.

HOW TO MAKE A FORAGED ROSE COCKTAIL

There are few things the forager loves more than an invasive species; the more you pick, the more virtuous you feel. *Rosa rugosa*, a salt-tolerant rose native to eastern Asia, has been making an increasing nuisance of itself on several continents after escaping from gardens where it is used to form a colourful hedge. It has taken over large areas of Europe, notably in coastal regions, and is also found extensively in North America and in the more urban reaches of Australasia. You may even have one in your garden.

Almost any rose, cultivated or wild, can be useful in the kitchen, but *Rosa rugosa* has two exceptional qualities – gorgeously fragrant petals and large hips ('hips' being the bright red fruits that form after the petals have fallen). The petals bear the quintessential perfume of roses, which lends itself to clear spirits like vodka, while the hips form the basis of a wonderful sweetener called rosehip syrup.

You will need:
small basketful of Rosa rugosa *petals*
bottle of vodka or eau de vie (fruit brandy)

small basketful of Rosa rugosa *hips*
water (enough to cover the rose hips)
caster sugar

Making rose petal spirit
Rosa rugosa has a long season and the plant continues to produce petals while other flowers set into hips. Pluck the petals from the green parts of the flower just as they are opening (to avoid the angry bee likely to be found inside). A small basketful of petals should be enough. Pack them inside a glass jar, pressing down gently. Put the lid on the jar and leave them at room temperature for 24 hours. Top up the jar with a good-quality vodka or eau de vie, put the top back on and leave for a week. Using a fine-mesh strainer or muslin, strain the liquor into sealable bottles, squeezing the petals so that no liquid is wasted. You won't know whether to drink this rose petal vodka or dab it behind your ears.

Making rosehip syrup
Wait for the hips to become red and ripe, then snap off enough to fill a small basket. Place in a medium-sized saucepan and fill it with just enough water to cover the hips. Boil them until the hips are soft. Gently mash the contents of the pan with a potato masher, then squeeze through a very fine mesh straining bag. Wash the bag and strain once more to ensure that none of the stomach-irritating hairs that adorn the seeds remain (children have long used rosehip seeds as itching powder). Heat the puree with a substantial amount of sugar – you can experiment with the amount, but a 1:1 sugar to puree ratio works well – and you will have rosehip syrup. It can be kept for two weeks in the fridge, or you can bottle and store or freeze it.

Making rose petal cocktails
Rose petal spirit is a bit of a trial to drink on its own, but wonderful in mixes and cocktails. I make a lot of wild cocktails, and I sometimes spray a glass with the rose petal vodka to give the whole thing a rosy perfume. Stirred into a chilled glass of your rosehip syrup, it is a summer evening treat.

The best summer cocktail I have ever tried (my own proud invention – you are welcome) is called a Pink Pint. I will leave the quantities to your own fine judgement, but the ingredients are: rose petal vodka, rosehip syrup, raspberry juice, lemonade (lemon-lime soda, for Americans), soda water and ice. Cheers!

HOW TO BREW WILD DANDELION AND MUSHROOM ALE

Come spring in North America's Appalachian Mountains, you'll find logs and stumps sprouting with wild oyster mushrooms and fields peppered with dandelions. A keen brewer can gather these up and turn their next home-brewed beer into a funky, citrusy, extraordinary libation.

But you don't have to be in Appalachia to try this recipe; these ingredients grow in abundance across the world. Dandelion greens (the stem and leaves) have a bittering quality that give this beer a higher perceived bitterness, to which their flowers add a floral punch. Oyster mushrooms engage the full palate and give this beer an interesting woody character.

Note that you should be fairly familiar with the art of brewing before trying this recipe.

You will need:
230 g (8 oz) dandelions, flowers separated from the stems
340 g (12 oz) oyster mushrooms
3.6 kg (8 lb) pilsner malt
900 g (2 lb) wheat malt
900 g (2 lb) spelt malt
230 g (8 oz) raw wheat
115 g (4 oz) acidulated malt
230 g (8 oz) rice hulls
¼ oz Columbus hops (15.5%AA)
1 whirlfloc tablet
140 g (5 oz) crushed Himalayan rock salt
1 pack White Labs yeast nutrient
1 vial of The Yeast Bay "Wallonian Farmhouse ale yeast"
180 g (6 oz) priming sugar
1 pack (5 g) champagne yeast

Before you begin brewing, separate the dandelion flowers from the greens, wash and thinly slice the mushrooms and take the yeast out of the fridge and bring it to room temperature.

Mash in your grist (grains), rice hulls and dandelion greens to a resting temperature of 68°C (154°F). Dandelion greens will add a bittering quality (much like hops) to your brew, and using them in the mash will stop them developing vegetable qualities that exposing them to boiling temperatures would bring on. Rest for 45 minutes.

Sparge at 76°C (169°F).

Collect 26 litres (7 gal) of wort (mashing liquid) in the boil kettle and bring to a boil. Boil for a total of 75 minutes. You'll need to pay close attention to the time at this stage. Add in the hops at 10 minutes; the whirlfloc at 55 minutes; the rock salt at 65 minutes; and the yeast nutrient at 70 minutes.

Place oyster mushrooms and dandelion flowers in a hop bag. Extinguish the flame on the boil kettle, then add the bag of mushrooms and dandelion flowers to the kettle.

Whirlpool the mixture, then add an immersion chiller and let sit for 15 minutes before starting to cool.

Cool wort down to 21°C (70°F) with an immersion chiller.

Rack with sterile syphon into a sterile carboy or food-grade bucket. Place lid on the carboy and shake to aerate for 5 minutes.

Add the vial of yeast. Shake for a further minute to mix.

Place sanitary airlock in the carboy and put in a cool area of your house with a black bag over it to block out UV light.

Allow to ferment for roughly two-and-a-half weeks, ideally at 22°C (72°F). It is helpful to place the carboy in a slightly warmer room after the first five days of fermentation to aid the yeast in the final phase of the ferment.

At the end of the ferment, when all bubbling has ceased from the airlock, transfer to a sterile bottling bucket. Add priming sugar and champagne yeast. Place in sterile bottles and store on their sides in a cool area for four weeks.

Serve at cellar temperature (18-23°C/64-73°F) in a tulip or wine glass with a platter of cheese or any kind of crustacean seafood.

Beer info:
OG 11.2 degrees Plato; FG 2.2 degrees Plato; 4.7% ABV; 12-15 IBU

DJ McCready, a brewer from Asheville, North Carolina, has worked at top breweries in the US and Australia. He now runs Bhutan's first craft brewery.

HOW (AND WHY) TO CAMP SUSTAINABLY

Camping offers opportunities to see and experience a new landscape, to forage from new fields and connect with local growers. It's possible to be even more sustainable on the road than it is at home, if you know how to pack and what to search for while you're out on adventures.

The experience of camping can change so much depending on how you do it. For us, the best camping experience comes when you totally immerse yourself in your environment, in the culture and nature around you – it makes for a much more sustainable experience.

It's about collecting food from where you are, both wild and locally produced, and choosing camp spots that are abundant with resources, like wood for your fire and water for your pot. It's about bringing the essential items with you so that you have everything you need to be comfortable, but leaving everything else behind so that you have to forage from the local landscape as you adventure through it.

Of course, sustainability isn't just about nature. It's about respecting the place you are visiting as a whole, which includes the people who live in it. The best way we've found to do this is to support local producers and buy fresh, local food from them. This food is always the best and it has no carbon miles attached to it. Plus you get to interact with local people who can help you identify good spots to fish, or to forage wild fruits or mushrooms. Support local communities and they'll support you.

When driving around, observe what is abundant around you, like crops, roadside stalls or local sourdough bakeries. There's almost always a local farmers market, usually on the weekend. And if you talk to locals, you'll often find someone with a verdant garden who will sell or trade you something! Keep your eyes peeled as you drive along too – food is all around us.

Camping sustainably is really that simple. If we don't respect the natural environment and the local people, enjoyable camping experiences will soon be a thing of the past. But respect both of these and we guarantee you and future campers will continue to wish you never had to go home.

Packing smart

Camping is a simple time, one made for getting back to basics. The only two essential tasks you need to worry about are gathering food … and then eating it! How we perform these two simple tasks makes all the difference between camping sustainably and just camping.

Food essentials

We bring just the basics and source the vast majority of our food locally. We always set out with:

- Some homemade passata.

- A jam or marmalade.

- Some pickled mixed vegetables and some fermented vegetables like dill pickles or kimchi (to keep our bellies healthy while we travel).

- Nuts and seeds.

- Pumpkin, potatoes, sweet potatoes, ginger, turmeric, garlic. These are versatile fresh foods that store super well for a long time without refrigeration and easily add flavour to so many different meals!

- Unrefined salt and pepper.

- Good olive oil for cooking.

We generally cook on the fire and it's super important to bring the right equipment for this; otherwise camp cooking can be a major time- and energy-sucker. It only takes a small fire to stay warm and if you have the right equipment, a small fire is all you'll need for cooking as well.

Equipment

There's no need to get too carried away and bring everything, including the kitchen sink, on the road. Again, camping should be a simple time. Here are a few essentials we always pack:

- Two stainless steel billies. As steel heats up fast, it is the most efficient vessel in which to boil water.

- A cast-iron frying pan and Dutch (camp) oven. Cast-iron stores heat; this is the most efficient way to capture your fire's peak energy when cooking more intensive meals.

- A thermos. This means you can make the day's tea/coffee and hot food on just one fire, whenever it suits you best – and keep it hot all day! We even have two small 330 ml (11 fl oz) thermoses for takeaway coffees on the go because they last a lifetime compared to regular reusable coffee cups.

- Coffee grinder and maker (plunger, Aeropress, stovetop – whatever you're into!).

- A good shovel. Your all-purpose camp tool for moving coals, digging toilet holes and a million other little tasks, but, most importantly, for burying all your compostable scraps to keep them out of landfill. Always bury toilet and food waste at least 20 centimetres (8 in) deep and away from water sources.

- A quality esky (cool box). Spend on this. A good esky will stay cold with just one bag of ice for up to a week!

Here's a tip: forget the soap. When you're done cooking, if you have a greasy pot, throw in some wood ash and water and leave it overnight. The combination of fat and ash will make soap overnight, which you can heat to do your dishes with in the morning.

Gathering the local abundance

Wild foods can vary greatly from place to place,* but some super-common things to look out for on the road are:

- Wild fennel. An awesome flavouring for soups, stews, etc.

- Wild apples, plums and figs. These look exactly the same as the regular ones, but are just growing wild!

- Blackberries and other wild berries. Make sure they haven't been sprayed. Roadsides invariably are, but deep bush is generally safe – just make sure there is no yellowing of the leaves, which is a sure sign you need to move on.

- Fish (and other game too, though fishing is by far the simplest way to gather wild meat).**

* Don't gather from the wild without the supervision of an experienced mentor.

** Make sure you get a fishing/game licence for the state you are in.

Matt and Lentil Purbrick live a sustainable life on their farm, growing and harvesting and planting in rhythm with nature's seasons (see page 181).

HOW TO LEAVE NO TRACE

The most important part of camping – of any outdoor activity, really – is ensuring you leave nature just as you found her. That means travelling carefully: driving and walking on already established paths to minimise damage; being mindful about where you're going; taking your gear and rubbish away with you when you leave; and replacing anything you moved around. It's as simple as it sounds, but here are a few guidelines for successfully following the 'leave no trace' manifesto.

When hiking, plan your route and prepare properly for the terrain you will encounter. Knowing where you're heading means it's less likely you'll have to go off the established path. When hiking, don't spit seeds onto the ground or pick any flowers – anything that changes the natural environment is best avoided.

Set up your campsite on an already established spot. If that's not possible, choose a site that has already been cleared of vegetation and a few metres away from a water source to avoid contaminating the water with your washing up or personal care. If you use any rocks to anchor your tent, replace them when you leave.

Organise your food in advance so you have only exactly what you need; this way, you won't have to cart out much food waste, and you'll be less likely to leave something behind (see *How to pack for a car camping trip* on page 239).

Use existing fire pits where possible and keep your fire small. Be careful with campfires – set up the fire properly within a fire ring, make sure someone is always watching the fire and that it stays small and manageable. When you leave the campsite, ensure the fire is properly extinguished (see *How to build a campfire* on page 246).

Don't wash your kitchenware in the nearby water source – if you do need to use the water, collect some from the creek, river or lake and take it back to your campsite. Most leave no trace manifestos say not to bathe in a river or lake, but if you do want to freshen up in a water source, do it without soap, which is a chemical product that will contaminate the water. Make sure you're around 50 m (164 ft) away from any rivers, lakes or oceans when using water containing soap or waste. Scatter the water around your campsite when you're done to ensure none of it runs into the water source.

Dispose of all human waste properly – that means away from water, buried deep in the ground. The further away from water, the better, as water contaminated by human waste leads to diseases like Giardia. Bury your toilet paper with the waste, but take any tampons or pads out with you.

Admire wildlife from a distance rather than giving them food or attention. Make sure to lock up your perishables and put them in a place that animals can't reach, otherwise you risk them trashing your campsite in search of food.

Walk in – and out – with a clean tent. Brushing down your tent and your shoes before you leave avoids passing soil-borne diseases from place to place.

Before you leave, thoroughly check the campsite for any trace of your visit. Collect rubbish that other, less vigilant campers may have left behind.

Acknowledgements

A huge thank you to our contributors, whose words and images make up this book. Each and every story has brought us joy and inspiration. It's been a delightfully rewarding process working with all of you.

Thank you to our talented and articulate writer/editor, Lauren Whybrow, for being such a positive force and setting the tone for the book from the beginning.

Thank you to our project editor, Kate Armstrong, for being so passionate about this project and meticulously crafting the book's pages with creativity and flair.

Big thanks to the team at Hardie Grant, in particular Melissa Kayser, for believing in us and allowing us to create this book.

Thanks to designer Kåre Martens, typesetter Megan Ellis and the whole Hardie Grant design team for bearing with us and creating such stunning work. Thank you also to the uber-talented Bec Kilpatrick for the illustrations. Bec and her partner Andrew Pavlidis' photos are a big part of what made this book so beautiful.

Thank you to our friends and family for their continual support and encouragement since launching Homecamp.

And finally, thank you to our daughter Anais, a true little outdoor adventurer, for reminding us to enjoy the simple things in life.

..........x

Published in 2017 by Hardie Grant Travel, a division of Hardie Grant Publishing

Hardie Grant Travel (Melbourne)
Building 1, 658 Church Street
Richmond, Victoria 3121

Hardie Grant Travel (Sydney)
Level 7, 45 Jones Street
Ultimo, NSW 2007

hardiegranttravel.com

Explore Australia is an imprint of Hardie Grant Travel

A Cataloguing-in-Publication entry is available from the catalogue of the National Library of Australia at www.nla.gov.au

Homecamp
ISBN 9781741175035

Recipes disclaimer: All recipes use Australian measurements, such as 20 ml tablespoons and 250 ml cups.

Photography credits:
All images shown within each story © the story's author, except for the following: Front endpaper Brooke Holm; back endpaper Bec Kilpatrick & Andrew Pavlidis; ii–v Bec Kilpatrick & Andrew Pavlidis; vii–viii Hilary Walker; ix Bec Kilpatrick & Andrew Pavlidis; x–1 Brooke Holm; 2–3 Daniel Wakefield Pasley; 8–9 Ben Leshchinsky; 16 & 18 Angus Kennedy; 20–21 Andy Summons; 36–37 The Adventure Handbook; 52–53 Ben Leshchinsky; 60 Vladimir Serov/ Blend/imagefolk; 62–63 Andrew Pavlidis; 65 Rachel Kay Photography; 66–67 Vic Phillips; 68 (from top) Jonathan Cherry, Melissa Parsons; 70–71 Vic Phillips; 72–73 Brooke Holm; 86–87 Jackson Loria; 88 500px/imagefolk; 91–92 Cat Vinton; 92–93 Dmitry Rukhlenko/Cultura RM/imagefolk; 95 Andrew Pavlidis; 96–97 Ben Leshchinsky; 100 Paul Gablonski; 106–107 Andrew Pavlidis; 130–131 Daniel Wakefield Pasley; 162–163 Andrew Pavlidis; 164–168 Luisa Brimble; 170–171 Andrew Pavlidis; 178–179 Brook Holm; 180, 182 & 186–187: Shantanu Starick; 199–201 Charlie Kinross; 209 Kate J. Armstrong; 210–211 Ben Leshchinsky; 230–231 Bec Kilpatrick; 236–237 Andrew Pavlidis; 260–261 Bec Kilpatrick & Andrew Pavlidis

Commissioning editor
Melissa Kayser

Managing editor
Marg Bowman

Project & text editor
Kate J. Armstrong

Writer & contributing editor
Lauren Whybrow

Proofreader
Michael Ryan

Designer
Kåre Martens, HANDVERK

Design Manager
Mark Campbell

Production Manager
Todd Rechner

Typesetter
Megan Ellis

Pre-press
Megan Ellis and Splitting Image Colour Studio

Printed in China by 1010 Printing International Limited